lives
& times
of hrh

lives & times of hrh

herman ronald hochstadt

RIDGE BOOKS
SINGAPORE

Published under the Ridge Books imprint by:

NUS Press
National University of Singapore
AS3-01-02, 3 Arts Link
Singapore 117569

Fax: (65) 6774-0652
E-mail: nusbooks@nus.edu.sg
Website: http://nuspress.nus.edu.sg

ISBN 978-981-325-119-9 (case)

National Library Board, Singapore Cataloguing in Publication Data

Name(s): Hochstadt, Herman Ronald.
Title: Lives & times of hrh / Herman Ronald Hochstadt.
Other title(s): Lives & times of Herman Ronald Hochstadt
Description: Singapore : NUS Press, [2020]
Identifier(s): OCN 1145094149 | ISBN 978-981-325-119-9 (hardback)
Subject(s): LCSH: Hochstadt, Herman Ronald. | Civil service--Singapore--Biography. | Singapore--Officials and employees--Biography. | Singapore--History--20th century.
Classification: DDC 352.63092--dc23

Typeset by: Ogma Solutions Pvt Ltd
Printed by: Markono Print Media Pte Ltd

Dedicated
to
Karen Lynn & Erwin Wei-Sung

Contents

Foreword

I thank my good friend, Herman Hochstadt, for giving me the honour of writing the foreword of his memoirs. I first met Herman in 1957, when I entered the University of Malaya, in Singapore, as a freshman, to study law. Herman was several years ahead of me. I have therefore known Herman since 1957, a span of sixty-three years.

Outstanding Eurasians

The Eurasian community is one of the smallest in Singapore. It has, nevertheless, produced an outstanding President, Dr Benjamin Sheares; an outstanding Law Minister, Eddie Barker; and three Permanent Secretaries, Stanley Stewart, George Bogaars and Herman Hochstadt.

Herman Hochstadt graduated from the University of Malaya, in 1958, with a very good honours degree in philosophy. He joined the Administrative Service in 1959 and retired from the service in 1989, just three months short of his 56th birthday. During those thirty eventful years, he had the privilege of working for Mr Lee Kuan Yew, Dr Goh Keng Swee and Mr Eddie Barker. He had served as the Permanent Secretary of the Ministries of Communications, Education, Finance and Law, and held senior positions in the

Ministries of Finance, Foreign Affairs and Interior & Defence and in the Monetary Authority of Singapore.

Herman's contributions

What were some of Herman's most important contributions?

First, he implemented the government's decision to accord equal pay for female civil servants.

Second, he served as Secretary to Prime Minister Lee Kuan Yew from 1962 to 1965. He witnessed history in the making, for example, when Singapore joined Malaya, Sabah and Sarawak to form Malaysia, in 1963 and the separation in 1965.

Third, he was the Administrative Secretary of the Singapore delegation, led by Dr Toh Chin Chye and included Mr S Rajaratnam, to seek admission to the United Nations in September 1965 and, from New York, to embark on a two month tour of countries around the world, to seek recognition of the new Republic of Singapore and gain general goodwill.

Fourth, he was the first Director of Manpower, of the infant Ministry of Interior & Defence, and played an important role in building up that Ministry and the Singapore Armed Forces.

Fifth, he was at the Ministry of Communications, when Prime Minister Lee overruled the Ministry, and decided to build the new airport at Changi, instead of expanding Paya Lebar airport.

Sixth, he was the first Permanent Secretary of the Ministry of Education who made weekly visits to the schools and who sought the opinions of the principals and teachers, to assist in the formulation of policies.

Seventh, he was a very effective and popular Permanent Secretary (Finance) (Budget) of the Ministry of Finance. It is due to leaders like Herman that Singapore has enjoyed fiscal prudence and sound monetary policy.

Three Humorous Incidents

The book is full of humour. Let me give three examples. At the dinner in New Delhi, hosted by Prime Minister of India, Indira Gandhi, for the Singapore delegation, Herman found to his embarrassment that the zip in his pants had given way. To hide the problem, Herman tucked a napkin into his trousers to cover his gaping zipper. The leader of the Singapore delegation, Toh Chin Chye, noticed this when they had to stand for the toasts and berated Herman after the banquet.

The second funny incident happened in Tunis, Tunisia. Dr Toh Chin Chye had ordered a cup of Turkish coffee at their hotel. When the coffee arrived, Dr Toh was angry with its small size. He picked it up and emptied the whole content into his mouth. He immediately spat the whole thing out, showering the people at the table with the coffee debris.

The third funny incident happened in Moscow. Two Russians, a man and a woman, at the hotel where the delegation was staying, must have mistakenly thought, from his looks, that Herman was Russian. Each spoke on different occasions to Herman in Russian. Only to get, "nyet", Russian for no and one of the few Russian words Herman knew, in return. This made the Russian man and woman, on each occasion, most upset. Most likely, each was expecting yes in return and got a no instead.

Non-Resident Ambassador

After leaving the civil service, Herman had a very successful career in the private sector and in public service. He served as our Non-Resident Ambassador/High Commissioner to Mauritius, Tanzania, South Africa, Namibia, Botswana and Swaziland, with great distinction. Earlier in his career, Herman joined the newly established Ministry of Foreign Affairs. He was going to be posted to our Embassy in Washington, as the Deputy Chief of Mission. However, for no officially declared reason but only surmise that it was owing to envy in the Ministry and the fact that he is an Eurasian, the posting order was speedily rescinded.

Escaping Death Twice

Herman had two narrow escapes with death. In the first case, he was flying from Singapore to the United States. He was booked on a flight from Singapore to Los Angeles, with a transit stop in Taipei. But he changed to a flight to San Francisco instead, with a transit in Hong Kong. The SQ plane crashed at the airport in Taipei. In the second case, he was flying back to Singapore from Jakarta. The plane was late. The station manager offered him a seat on a Silk Air flight. Fortunately, Herman declined because that Silk Air plane crashed and killed everyone on board.

Conclusion

My wife has always told me that a man's most precious asset is his reputation. Herman Hochstadt has an excellent reputation. He was a good husband of Peggy Leong. He is a good father of Karen and Erwin. He is a loyal and steadfast friend. He is a good and caring boss. He is a man of integrity. He has served Singapore, with great distinction, both in the private and public sectors.

Tommy Koh

Preface

For such a long time it seemed I was often accosted and at times and on occasion interrogated as to when and why, if not, an autobiography or biography of mine would appear. Then coaxed, cajoled and prodded when I replied there were no plans nor any intention on my part for an autobiography or biography of mine to appear in print. They would insist that the how, why and wherefore of my forebears coming to this part of the world and settling in Singapore from around the time of Raffles' Singapore and, furthermore, the story of my own life and service of some thirty years in and for the government of Singapore was an essential part of the story, if not history, of Singapore itself and did not in fact really belong to me but to all Singaporeans and Singapore, and it was my duty therefore to ensure its record and dissemination for the present and for posterity. My very good friend from our days of some half-century before in the then University of Malaya in Singapore at Bukit Timah, Haider M Sithawalla, kindly offered to commission a good writer to ghost write my autobiography or write my biography if I preferred, and threatened to go ahead and get either accomplished himself when I politely demurred.

The thirty or so years of my government service or servitude as some friends were wont to proclaim, ran but oft times sprinted from 1959 when the then Colony of Singapore under domination of the United Kingdom of Great Britain, Ireland, Scotland and Wales, morphed into the State of Singapore internally independent but still dominated in regard to defence and foreign relations by the UK, which in fact continued for another eight or so years to maintain in Singapore an air, land and sea defence capability, including its largest naval base east of the Suez; to 1963 when the State of Singapore became a state in the newly created Malaysia out of the Federation of Malaya, State of Singapore and Borneo territories of Sabah and Sarawak; on to 1965 when Singapore seemed to pop out of Malaysia like a champagne cork, but minus any celebratory froth, to morph once more, this time into the newly independent and sovereign Republic of Singapore; and finally into the quarter-century or so leading up to my early retirement from service in and for the government of the Republic of Singapore in 1989 just about three months short of fifty-six years of age.

It would have been taboo and most possibly have brought the wrath of the Official Secrets Act (OSA) crashing upon my civil service head had I made or seriously attempted to make and maintain any inclusive record or notes of and about those thirty or so years of my service in and for the government of the Republic of Singapore. But without any such record or notes, no proper autobiography or biography was feasible. For, as everyone knows or should, an autobiography or a biography must regurgitate the facts: the truth, the whole truth and nothing but the truth. Hence my good friend Haider M Sithawalla was thanked profusely for his kind offer to find me a ghost writer, but my response regrettably had to be a firm "No!"

There were some who nevertheless persisted and kindly offered that perhaps some suitable alternative to either an autobiography or biography could be found that steered clear of the OSA. Hence the concept for and of a memoir was born. A memoir, unlike an autobiography or biography both of which should be dependent on and wholly reflective of complete and true records or notes, could well be and often is dependent on just memory and recall which might well fall short of being reflective of the truth, the whole truth. More so with age and infirmity affecting the mind. While a memoir did seem a solution, how to accommodate the seemingly several lives hrh appeared to have led at different times and circumstances remained a problem. Eureka: *lives & times of hrh*, a memoir!

For helping this publication exist at all, thanks must go to National University of Singapore President, Professor Tan Eng Chye. Without whose encouragement and support throughout the endeavour there would be no *lives & times of hrh*, and NUS Press would have one fewer publication. Any deficiencies of or in *lives & times of hrh* cannot and must not be attributed to him. My thanks too to Edi Fung and Dawn Loh Li-Min Tracy both of NUS Development Office for their quiet but strong and most encouraging support throughout.

The tedious but meticulous fact-checking and more in the backroom by Tim Yap Fuan and Han Ming Guang under direction of NUS University Librarian Lee Cheng Ean, or Ean, must be recognised. My thanks to both for their tedious backroom toil. And thanks too to Ng Boon Hwee also of NUS Libraries who, also under direction of Ean, most cheerfully and skillfully helped unjam either or both my laptops whenever needed, and unjam me too on occasion.

Peter Schoppert of NUS Press, many thanks for your vision that the family story from around the time of Raffles' Singapore and of my own life too from 1959, intertwined with the history of Singapore itself of those times could well be fit for publication by NUS Press. Not forgetting your promise at the very start to assign a good editor to nurture the story through to publication by NUS

Press. Which promise you did duly keep with your assignment of Lindsay Davis who toiled most assiduously and magically turned a wild and unruly thing into a manuscript fit enough for publication by the venerable NUS Press, which is known for usually publishing academic, sedate, serious and solemn treatises.

NUS University Librarian Lee Cheng Ean – Ean – and Ajith Prasad – Ajith or AP – latter my colleague of days some forty years ago at the Ministry of Finance (Budget Division), both most staunchly and stoutly stood beside, behind and at times even in front of me from gestation to birth and on to growth and development of *lives & times of hrh*. To both, my most sincere appreciation, gratitude and thanks.

My thanks in a bundle to be unravelled by members of the Treasury Coffee Club (TCC): Chris Liew, Dileep Nair, Henry Sim Cheng Tee and Ajith Prasad too who should not be left out now just because he came in for thanks earlier in a different capacity. Each and every one gave of their support individually or in a team or in teams and with encouragement and more that helped in no small measure to see the endeavour all the way through. No doubt George Edwin Bogaars, founder of the TCC, when Permanent Secretary (Finance) (Budget), would proudly smile from on high at how these TCC protégés of his have turned out.

Thanks of the highest order should and must go to Professor Tommy Koh and Gopinath Pillai – Gopi to me – both freshies of mine at the University of Malaya in Singapore at Bukit Timah a half-century ago. Prof Tommy Koh without hesitation most graciously promised a foreword for *lives & times of hrh*, a memoir, and duly delivered – even without contract. He also most kindly consented to be guest of honour at the book's launch and deliver, too, an address at the launch. To my very old and dear friend

Gopinath Pillai, very special thanks to you my old freshie friend for kindly agreeing to be event host at launch of *lives & times of hrh*.

There remain the unnamed who remain nameless for reasons of their own or owing to a far-from-dependable memory and recall, who gave freely of their advice, wisdom, encouragement and support without which there might not be *lives & times of hrh*, a memoir, to whom an immense debt of appreciation and gratitude and now most hopefully repaid in kind with my thanks a million!

hrh

I

The Hochstadt Family: Early History

My paternal great grandmother, Elizabeth, was said by my father, Henry David Hochstadt, to have been a fiery Irish-Indian lady with flaming red hair – passed down to my elder sister, Cora, and late younger brother, Carl – who, when she and her German husband, variously referred to as Philip Peter Hochstadt and Peter Philip, lived in India, cooked fiery hot curries for family meals. One anecdote recounts how a young son of Philip and Elizabeth invited a young neighbour, newly out from England to India, to the Hochstadt home for a family lunch one day. On putting the first spoonful of rice and curry into his mouth, the young English neighbour dropped his spoon, shot up from his seat, and dashed to his home next door. Mouth open wide to catch any cooling breeze as he ran, yelling as best he could through that wide, open mouth, "They eat fire! They eat fire!"

***

Philip Hochstadt was said – though not substantiated – to have first migrated to then British India from his home near Munich, in Bavaria, where there was and still is a town named Hochstadt – "hoch" meaning high and "stadt" meaning town. Why and for what purpose is a mystery. He might have been running away from someone, or something. Whomsoever or whatsoever it might have been, his escape to oblivion seems to have been effective. In India he met and settled down, though not for too long, with that fiery, red-headed Irish-Indian, Elizabeth. What he did for a living is a mystery. A daughter was born to Philip and Elizabeth in India. But Philip and Elizabeth moved on, with family in tow, to White Rajah Brooke's Sarawak. My paternal grandfather, John Hochstadt, was born in Kuching, Sarawak, in 1871. Peter, Elizabeth and family, moved on again to Singapore, then part of the Straits Settlements.

John Hochstadt, my paternal grandfather, became a marine engineer, in that age then of newfangled steamships. He rose to chief engineer, aboard coastal steamships, but decided to call it a day at sea, before the normal retirement age, and settled in Singapore. He jointly founded with his wife, Rosa Delphina D'Almeida, Singapore Casket Co Pte Ltd in 1920. Rosa Delphina was a granddaughter of Dr Jose D'Almeida, a ship surgeon turned businessman and trader in Singapore, in the era following Stamford Raffles' landing in 1819. His business enterprise was successful and became a family one too, with his sons joining in and helping run it. Testimony to that success is the naming of a street off Raffles Place, one-time Commercial Square, D'Almeida Street. Singapore newspaper reports of the time show the family of Jose D'Almeida led an active social life.

Rosa Delphina's father, William, was the son of Jose D'Almeida, and married Fatimah, a Malay lady. It is on record that Rosa Delphina married a De Wind before she must have settled down with John Hochstadt. John and Rosa had a daughter, Annie, who became a qualified nurse and midwife; another daughter, Flora; a third daughter, Marion (May); another daughter, Cornelia (Nellie);

daughter, Grace; then son, Henry David, my father; and finally, youngest daughter, Alice. My father did have an elder brother, Victor, who succumbed in his early twenties to tuberculosis – commonly referred to then as consumption – leaving my father to perpetuate the Hochstadt family name.

My father and mother, Lucy Beryl (Girlie) Phillips, had two daughters, Myrna and Cora, before I came along. All six of my parents' children were born at home. Annie, my father's eldest sister, being a qualified nurse and midwife, was in attendance for the births of the first five children but not the sixth and youngest. My youngest brother, John Philip, was born in Syonan-to in 2602 by Japanese reckoning, during World War II and the Japanese Occupation of Singapore. At the time, Aunt Annie was with her own daughter Flora and the latter's husband, Dr Xavier, in Sibu, Sarawak. Travel by boat across the South China Sea was difficult and hazardous then owing to the war. Flora or Flora Kechil (Little Flora), as she was called to distinguish her from her Aunt Flora, Aunt Annie's younger sister, had married Dr Xavier and they settled in Sibu, Sarawak, where Dr Xavier set up a medical practice.

An obituary in a local newspaper of the time, records the passing away of a Mrs Scully – wife of the chief clerk of the Penang High Court. She was a sister of my grandfather, John Hochstadt. That obituary also records Mrs Scully's and my grandfather's brother Herman, after whom I was named, and two sisters, living at the time in Detroit, Michigan, USA. My father did recount how his aunts, those two sisters of his father, during an extended visit to Singapore sometime after migrating to America, set up and ran the first dry cleaning enterprise in Singapore. No doubt they drew on what they had learnt and experienced in America for the enterprise. Newspaper advertisements of the day record my great grandfather, Philip Peter or Peter Philip Hochstadt, who must have been quite an entrepreneur, successful or not, offering milk for sale and also running a stable for horse-drawn cabs at Balestier Road. A site plan titled “Plan for STABLE AND OUTHOUSE, BALESTIER ROAD, 3ms”, dated 1895, lists the owner as P Hochstadt, and signed off, “P P Hochstadt”, is in the National Archives of Singapore. That site is in the vicinity of the Sun Yat Sen memorial museum in the Balestier Road area.

Although not from Hamburg himself, but Bavaria, my great grandfather, Philip Peter or Peter Philip Hochstadt’s German spirit of business enterprise might well be reflected in the report in *The Straits Observer*, 6 August 1875, of “… Young Germans educated in Hamburg … generally able to speak and write two or three different modern languages and … trained to a mercantile life” who, “it is not surprising … are enabled, in many instances, to compete successfully with men from England, who however accomplished in a classical sense, may not have been designed and prepared for commerce from their youth, as their German rivals.”

There are newspaper reports too of those times of various Hochstadt family members’ social and not-so-social activities. One such not-so-social activity reported, was when a Charles Hochstadt was taken to court by his own mother for some misdemeanour. In court, however, his mother did not press charges. He was ordered to undergo observation and treatment at a mental institution. It appears his mother could well have made a plea to the court, in mitigation, that his misdemeanour was occasioned by the full moon.

That plea could, perhaps, indicate a direct family link to a person variously named, “Holstadt”, “Hochstead”, “Hochsteadt” and “Hochstadt”, in the *Diary of Mr W. Pretyman (Resident at Tumpassak Borneo) May 2nd 1878 to Feb 5th 1880*. That “Holstadt”, “Hochstead”, “Hochsteadt” or “Hochstadt” too, claimed in mitigation for his misdemeanour in letting pistol shots off into the air at his residency camp at Tumpassak, that the full moon was to blame for his misdemeanour.

A grand uncle of mine, Charles Hochstadt, younger brother of my grandfather John Hochstadt, was a lighthouse keeper who, at one time, kept lighthouse off Miri, Sarawak. He took up with a local Iban lady, possibly, who bore him children – one reportedly a handsome and muscular young lad, with family name Hochstadt. Charles Hochstadt must have abandoned that maybe Iban lady in Miri when he retired as lighthouse keeper there and took up residence in Singapore, in the early to mid 1950s, to live out his last days as a house guest in the living quarters of Singapore Casket Co, co-founded by his brother, John Hochstadt, who by then had been dead and gone for a decade.

My grandfather, John Hochstadt, was said by my father to have pursued a claim to property in Singapore confiscated by the British colonial authorities during World War I, for being owned by a German and hence deemed an enemy alien-owned property. It was never restored to ownership of my grandfather after World War I, though he resolutely pursued his claim to restoration of that property to ownership of the Hochstadt clan right up to the outbreak of World War II. When he and Grandma Rosa Delphina took refuge in living quarters at Casket Co on Lavender Street from 33 Chancery Lane where they then lived, he took with him an old seaman's metal trunk in which he kept his exchange of correspondence with the British Custodian of Enemy Alien Property. It was under his bed at Casket Co and supposedly still there till well after his death in 1943, at the age of 72. But the metal trunk and contents and other household clutter were, apparently, disposed of and disappeared when the Lavender Street premises of Singapore Casket Co underwent major upgrading and renovation in later years. A good friend of mine, the late Professor Lee Yong

Kiat, one-time official physician to Prime Minister Lee Kuan Yew, recounted finding, in the course of his own research into the history of King Edward VII College of Medicine, record in the National Archives of that pursuit by grandfather John Hochstadt of his claim to restoration of the confiscated property.

II

Pre-War Years and the Japanese Occupation

While managing Singapore Casket Co, my grandfather, John Hochstadt, was said to have put a half-bottle of brandy with a glass next to it on his desk in the office first thing in the morning when starting on his office work. He would take a stiff gulp of brandy neat from the glass as he worked, topping up the glass whenever needed throughout his working day, with a short break for lunch in the office followed by a brief afternoon snooze. That bottle of brandy would be finished before the end of each working day. Singapore Casket Co was located then at Prinsep Street – that part of the street later became part of Selegie Road – on the ground floor of which was the office and work area and on the upper floor living quarters for the family. *A Nonya Mosaic: My Mother's Childhood* by Gwee Thin Hock, refers to the "Hochstadt family of Prinsep Street", with a boy in the family by name of "Henry Boy" and five sisters – it should be six – named "Annie, May, Nellie, Grace and Alice" – Flora was left out.

My father grew up there and went to St Joseph's Institution, a comfortable walking distance away, as was the Catholic Cathedral of the Good Shepherd, diagonally opposite St Joseph's Institution, across Bras Basah Road. The surrounding area, including Queen Street, was a haven for Eurasians then, to live in and play around. My father had a great friend, Kenny Mosbergen, from a prominent Eurasian family, who were stalwarts of the Roman Catholic Church, and themselves lived at Queen Street. My father used to recount how Kenny Mosbergen and he went on long walks around Singapore and even to Woodlands where the Causeway to Johore was then under construction. They used to hop from large granite block to large granite block, laid there in the Straits of Johor as foundation for the Causeway, as far out as they could go, then hop back to Woodlands. Because of my father's close association with Eurasians then, he grew up in the firm belief he was a pukka Eurasian himself, and always considered himself to be one.

My Aunt Annie married a man with the family name Vickery, who was the father of the Flora Kechil who went to live in Sibu, Sarawak, with her husband, Dr Xavier and develop their family. Vickery was employed by the Straits Trading Company that then had a tin smelting plant. It was told in the family of how Vickery, while on duty on one of his rounds of the tin smelting plant, slipped while walking along the narrow gangway around the brim of a large storage vat of hot smelted tin. He plunged right in and was fished out, as quickly as possible, unconscious. He was rushed to hospital, but succumbed there to his extensive and terrible burns, twenty-four hours, or thereabouts, later. Surviving even a day after such a catastrophic accident was a testimony to the giant of a man he was said to have been, in build and the determination and will to survive! Aunt Annie, who was still quite young then, never remarried and mourned her loss to her last days. Despite her personal tragedy, she was always the good Samaritan in helping to nurse extended family members and midwifing for babies of those who called on her for help.

Singapore Casket Co business was good enough for Grandpa John Hochstadt to move the business from the work-cum-living-quarters premises at Prinsep Street to a commercial premises at 129/131 Lavender Street – later extended to the adjoining property to become 129–133. The Lavender Street area was then a newly developed estate for small industries, which were then just emerging in Singapore. It was near a river estuary and small table vegetable farms. The vegetable farms in the Lavender Street area used human waste or nightsoil for fertiliser, that gave off quite a stench. Hence, declared wags of the time in derision, the street named Lavender, after the sweet-smelling lavender itself!

Grandpa John Hochstadt also, around then, bought a large two storey house at 33 Chancery Lane, a prime residential location in Singapore, for he and family to live in, plus extended family, including his daughter Marion, son-in-law Charles (Carlo) Burton Webb as well as their daughter and three sons. And, of course, for visiting relatives from wherever and whenever were welcome, as well, to stay and make themselves comfortable to their hearts' content while in Singapore.

The main, double-storey building at Chancery Lane, in which the family lived, was on a hillock at the front of the block. A smaller hillock was behind, on which was a smaller, single-storey building where the main kitchen was as well as quarters for the servants, gardeners and syces. A wide flight of brick and mortar stairs connected the two hillocks and their respective buildings. In the first bombing of Singapore by the Japanese at the start of World War II in the Pacific, a bomb was dropped on the second hillock. The house and grounds were most probably not the target, more than likely, the bomb was intended for Government House, not too far away, where the then British governor of colonial Singapore lived. The damage, as far as that Hochstadt home went, was done.

Grandpa John Hochstadt, Grandma Rosa Delphina and their grandson, Augustus (Guy) Webb – second son of Uncle Carlo and Aunt May Webb – packed their bags and *barang-barang* and moved, with a cook and a couple of servants, to the Singapore Casket Co premises at 129/131 Lavender Street, following hasty work to create habitable living quarters for all there.

My Uncle Carlo, who was a captain in the Singapore Volunteer Corps (SVC) and on active service as such, was taken prisoner of war (POW) by the invading Japanese forces. He was sent to work on the Siam-Burma Death Railway, but survived. After World War II, he was sent for recuperation to Perth, Western Australia, where his wife, May, and third and youngest son, Hugh, had been since they were evacuated from Singapore at the outbreak of war. On his and his family's return to Singapore, my Uncle Carlo Webb, took up appointment as managing director of Singapore Casket Co. My Grandpa John Hochstadt and Grandma Rosa Delphina, had both passed away by then, during the Japanese Occupation. Uncle Carlo's eldest son, Gordon, had been in Western Australia from just before the outbreak of World War II following his enlistment in the Royal Australian Air Force (RAAF) and assignment in Australia. Uncle Carlo's daughter Pearl, and the eldest of his children, had married a jockey from Queensland, Australia, Skeets Garrad, who had worked at the Singapore Turf Club before the outbreak of the war. She went with Garrad to Queensland, when he returned there from Singapore. The second son, Augustus (Guy) Webb, worked in Singapore Casket Co, assisting Grandpa John Hochstadt, and later Grandma Rosa Delphina when Grandpa John Hochstadt passed away, in managing the company, in the absence of Carlo, who had been general manager before the war.

Guy was taken into custody by the feared Kempeitai, or Japanese Military Police. He was held for some six months during which he was tortured, but survived and was freed. After the war, he entered the King Edward VII College of Medicine but, in his second year there, left on getting married to his wartime sweetheart, Zita Beck, and went back to Singapore Casket Co as assistant to his father, who had returned as managing director. After his father retired, and went to live in Queensland with Pearl, Guy took over as managing director.

My maternal grandfather, John Phillips, who was from Liverpool, England, ran away to sea as a boy to sign on as apprentice cabin boy, and rose over time to become captain of a coastal steamship. He was taken POW, when he surrendered himself soon after the fall of Singapore. Grandpa John Phillips usually stayed with his wife, Helen Marcus, and my parents and family at 14 Parkstone Road, when on shore leave. Both, Grandpa John Phillips and Grandma Helen, were at home with us when colonial Britain surrendered Singapore to Imperial Japan. As was their third son, my Uncle Stanley Phillips, following the evacuation of his family from Pulau Bukom, where he worked with the Shell Company and lived in the company's quarters. His wife, Marjorie Jumbu, my Aunt Marje, and their daughter, Bubbles, as we always called her, as well as Aunt Marje's mother and sister, took refuge with the nuns at the Convent of the Holy Infant Jesus on Queen Street.

The Singapore local population had been ordered by the British colonial authorities to build their own bomb shelters at the outbreak of the war. My father tried but gave up. He had tried to dig a trench for the shelter in the vacant land adjacent to the house but got down just a couple of feet when the water kept flowing into the trench in that low-lying land with a relatively high water table. So, he resorted to putting a sturdy teak dining table, that could seat eight diners in comfort, into the former servants' room on the ground level of the house, covered on top with a thick coconut coir mattress and a couple of thick, heavy duty blankets thrown over the lot. We kids would be ordered to run and hide under the table when the warning siren wailed, and while away the time playing card or board games or just making noise and quarrelling, till the all-clear siren sounded. The grown-ups did not usually get under that bomb shelter table but continued doing their own things. Our valve radio set kept us informed of the outside world, with Radio Nerom keeping us reasonably happy with its catchy tunes – first thing every morning, "Good morning, good morning…". Till it sadly went off the air when Singapore surrendered to the Japanese invading forces.

We knew our table bomb shelter would not save us from a direct bomb hit. But my father told us not to worry, since any direct hit on any bomb shelter would be an act of God, which no bomb shelter could survive. And when the shells flew overhead in those last days before the fall of Singapore, we were told not to worry if we heard the shells screaming overhead as that meant they were going by and not coming at us. Then, when the sky to the north was lit up at night and stayed lit for night after night, my Uncle Stanley surmised from the direction of the light that it was from the burning of oil tanks at the large oil installation of the Shell Company on Pulau Bukom, in an attempt to scotch those valuable resources before the Japanese forces could take them over and that, therefore, the battle for Singapore was most likely soon to end. How right he was. The British forces under General Percival surrendered unconditionally to the invading army of Japanese General Tomoyuki Yamashita, the Tiger of Malaya.

Following the surrender, households were notified that teams of Japanese soldiers, led by officers, would visit every house in the area, many of which had been vacated during the war when the occupants evacuated Singapore or took refuge elsewhere. On the appointed day for the visit to our area, my Grandpa John Phillips and his wife Grandma Helen, my Uncle Stanley, my parents, sisters, Myrna, Cora and Joan as well as my brother Carl and I were all assembled in that bomb shelter room, awaiting the dreaded visit. A Japanese officer, accompanied by about half a dozen of his soldiers, came into the room. The officer spoke English – my Uncle Stanley later said that officer had probably studied or trained in the US as he spoke with an American accent and had enquired about "gasoline" rather than the English "petrol" we were used to. The officer first asked if there was anyone English or from England amongst us. When my Grandpa John Phillips said that he was, the officer told him to report to and surrender himself at the nearest police station. The officer then asked for provisions to take away to feed his hungry men. My father pointed to a less than half-filled gunny sack of uncooked rice grains, strategically placed against a wall in the room – earlier my father had cunningly hidden away his store of rice grains and canned provisions for the family in the ceiling of one of the rooms on the main upper level of the house. Through hand gestures and basic English, my father tried to put across to the Japanese team that the rice was to feed the small children of the house who would go hungry and starve should their small store of rice be taken away. The officer seemed to relent. He then asked for gasoline. My father told the officer there was none and even the tank of my father's car, in the garage outside, was empty. The officer ordered two of his men to go to the garage to check, taking my father and his car key with them. According to what my father told us later, the two men checked the fuel gauge on the car's dashboard and saw the tank was empty. My father had shrewdly siphoned all the fuel in the car's tank to a portable storage tank and hidden it under a thick palm bush on the vacant land adjacent to the house. They then tried to start the car with my father's ignition key but could not – my father had also earlier taken out the rotor arm from the car's ignition system and hidden that away. So, the two soldiers gave up and returned the car key to my father. The two soldiers went back to the bomb shelter room, accompanied by my father, to report to their officer in Japanese. Shortly after which, the Japanese officer and his men left.

When Grandpa John Phillips surrendered himself, to be taken POW, he bade farewell to Grandma Helen, my mother Beryl Lucy (Girlie) and my siblings. I had been asked by my father to accompany Grandpa John Phillips and my Uncle Stan, in the car driven by my father, from 14 Parkstone Road to Joo Chiat Police Station, on East Coast Road not too far away, where Grandpa John Phillips was to surrender himself. When we got to Joo Chiat Police Station, my father stopped the car across from the main entrance to Joo Chiat Police Station along East Coast Road. Grandpa John Phillips bade farewell to his son, my Uncle Stanley, my father and me, then alighted from the car and briskly walked across East Coast Road, bereft of traffic then, and strode onto the sandy pathway, lined on either side with white-washed bricks, standing diagonally against each other on their narrower sides, on the grassy patch in front of the police station. When he got to the steps leading into the main foyer of the police station, he walked firmly to the top of the steps, walked straight in through the main foyer and was soon lost to our sight, in the dimness within. That was the last time I ever saw Grandpa John Phillips alive. Next time I saw him, was as a corpse in the mortuary of Singapore General Hospital off Outram Road. He had passed away in the POW wing of that hospital, following a fall while trying to get to the toilet after an operation for acute appendicitis.

My uncles Arthur and Stanley were, a little later, also taken POW, in response to a public call for all children of British nationals to surrender themselves. Their elder brother, my Uncle Sonny, was excused owing to a bad limp he suffered following a severe bout of rheumatic fever in his youth. During the Japanese Occupation of Singapore, he served as mandore or overseer of a team of anti-malarial labourers whose job was to daily scour less urban areas of Singapore to locate and destroy mosquitos and their habitats and breeding grounds and keep malaria, which was quite prevalent then and a dreaded scourge, at bay. Both my uncles Arthur and Stanley survived incarceration as POWs and returned to their families and old jobs too, after World War II.

Uncle Arthur was a teacher at St Patrick's School before the war and a much-respected one of mathematics. As well as a much sought-after tutor of mathematics, which he undertook only as a special favour and for free, for a very few select and deserving cases whom he thought could and would really benefit from his personal effort and sacrifice of time with his own family who meant the world to him. In fact, in my own case, after resuming my schooling in St Andrew's School post World War II, I fared badly in my maths examinations, mainly owing to having missed out on the very basics of maths at secondary school level. My mother was very concerned and appealed to her brother, my Uncle Arthur, for help. Uncle Arthur agreed and insisted I spend the entire year-end school vacation at his home with his four sons – Jack Arthur or Jackie, who was nearest to me in age and closest to me personally and with whom I got on very well; Clive, his second son, a few years younger than Jackie; Alphonso or Alfie; and Dennis. I was most happy to do so, hoping to be out playing with the four brothers the entire day, every day. But Uncle Arthur set a very firm timetable for me: for a couple of hours each morning he tutored me in elementary maths from the very basics up, then he set some exercises directly related to what I had just been tutored in, for me to work on myself while he and his wife, my Aunt Virginia or Ginnie, went off on some errand. When he got back, he expected to find the exercises he had set completed or nearly so, before he would release me to go out and play with his sons.

At the end of that long year-end school vacation, Uncle Arthur insisted I should continue with the tutoring at his home every weekend during school term, following the same schedule he had set during the year-end holiday. I used to cycle, during school term, every Friday afternoon after school, from 14 Parkstone Road to my Uncle Arthur's home, several miles away, at Jalan Pasir (later Sennett Road), off Upper East Coast Road. Jalan Pasir was then a sandy lane (as its name implies) that led up a steep hill. I used to cycle up that hill as far as I could, then dismount and push the bicycle the rest of the way to the top of the hill, remount and then cycle the remaining branch of the road to the right to my Uncle Arthur's home. On Sunday evenings, I would cycle back home and it would be a breeze coasting downhill. This continued, every weekend during school term, till I sat for my Cambridge School Certificate in which I scored an A for elementary mathematics, thanks to Uncle Arthur. My mother was most grateful and thanked her brother profusely, for not only helping me get through my maths in the Cambridge School Certificate, but even scoring an A. Uncle Arthur, just smiled and told my mother that if I did not have what it took, and were not intelligent and diligent enough, it would not have been possible. He only had to drill in the basics, so essential in mathematics. The rest was up to me. He gave me the confidence, perhaps over-confidence, to take pure mathematics for my BA (Pass) at university. But his faith probably gave me more confidence in my aptitude and ability in mathematics above the secondary school level than was warranted.

My mother was not taken POW by the Japanese during the occupation of Singapore. Immediately after the call to children of British nationals to surrender themselves, during which uncles Arthur and Stanley did as commanded, my father decided to go to the Registry of Births & Deaths to get an extract of his birth registration to take to the Japanese Civil Administrator of Singapore, Mamoru Shinozaki, to plead for exemption for my mother from the call, in view of her being married to a Eurasian. He went to the Registry and called on the registrar, whom he knew personally. They both searched for the record of my father's birth under the Asian category, which Eurasians would fall under as had been prescribed by the British colonial masters of Singapore. But could not find it. The registrar then suggested looking under the European category. Which they did, and they immediately found it! My father had indeed been registered under the European category, as German, being born of a German father. So, my father took the extract of his birth certificate to Mamoru Shinozaki, to plead on behalf of his wife for her exemption from incarceration as a POW, on grounds she was married to a German. And, as everyone knew then or should have known, the Germans were allies of the Japanese and on the same side in World War II. According to my father, Shinozaki was about to give an endorsement for my mother's exemption, when he paused, turned, and looked directly at my father and into his eyes and asked, "Were you interned as a POW by the British earlier?" My father said he was nonplussed by the question and was pondering how best to respond, when Shinozaki apparently had a change of mind, laughed, and said, "Never mind!" And gave the endorsement. So, my mother was never interned as a POW.

But my mother's mother, Grandma Helen, was interned in the last few months of the war. From almost the start of the Japanese

Occupation, a Star of David-like emblem, printed on cardboard, had been issued to be affixed to some prominent feature on the front of our home. It was said to be issued to spouses, and designated others, of Britishers and other enemy aliens. The one issued for Grandma Helen had been fixed by my father to a wooden pillar at the top of the steps leading to the veranda at the front of our home. Grandma Helen suffered a stroke and was paralysed and confined to bed in the last year or so of World War II. When the call came in the last few months of the war for women, such as her, married to Britishers to be taken POW as well, we had expected that since Grandma Helen had by then been paralysed because of her stroke, she would be exempted. But she was not. One afternoon an open lorry pulled into the driveway of 14 Parkstone Road, with an armed Japanese guard beside the driver, and a couple of labourers in the back. The labourers got down to carry Grandma Helen into the back of the lorry, to lie there on the bare, hard floorboards, open to the sky and blazing sun. The lorry then drove off, with the workers sitting in the back with Grandma Helen. We were fearfully suspicious Grandma Helen's few possessions and the little cash in Japanese "banana notes" my mother had packed to be taken with her to POW camp, would be lost to those two labourers, from the looks they gave each other when they realised Grandma Helen was paralysed and could not even complain, having lost the power of speech.

My Uncle Stanley who happened to be in the POW detail assigned to the main entrance of the POW camp at Sime Road to help in the unloading of lorries arriving at the camp, later reported he had not seen any possessions accompanying Grandma Helen when she entered the POW camp at Sime Road that day. He had helped to carry her down from the lorry and into the camp and was so sad to see her in such a pitiful state, speechless and with tears streaming down her cheeks when she saw and recognised Uncle Stanley. She died in the Sime Road POW camp not long after.

During the Japanese Occupation, my father was asked by Dr C J Paglar, who had been designated by the powers that be amongst the Japanese overlords of Singapore, as a sort of official liaison between them and the Singapore Eurasian community, to lead a team of representative Eurasians on a mission to the Eurasian settlement at Bahau in the jungle of Negri Sembilan near Seremban. The Japanese had sought to establish a settlement there for the Eurasians of Singapore where the latter could grow their own food and thus help lessen the burden of provisioning the population at large of Singapore. Besides, the Eurasians of Singapore were suspect, owing to their part-European antecedence, as possible collaborators of the British and Allies in opposition to the Japanese Imperial Army, and it would be best if as many as possible could be relocated to some remote and desolate place far from Singapore. My father had known Dr Paglar from well before World War II. Dr Paglar had a well-known and popular medical practice at Joo Chiat Place, and was a big-game hunter of repute and good friend of the Sultan of Johor, who was also a keen big-game hunter. The Sultan and Dr Paglar used to hunt together in the jungles of Johor. Dr Paglar's mission to Bahau, was supposed to be a fact-finding one and the team was to give a report of their visit on their return to Singapore to motivate Eurasians from Singapore to move to Bahau. The team went by rail to Bahau and spent a night and day there before returning to Singapore by rail as well.

The report presented on return to Singapore was a glowing one, though my father claimed in private to have not approved nor even seen the report before it was published in the *Syonan Shimbun*. And, he believed, neither had the leader of the mission himself, Dr Paglar. My father contracted a very bad case of malaria during his brief sojourn to Bahau where malaria was very rampant then. He could not rid himself of that disease till many years after the end of World War II and many doses of quinine and other medication. When the disease did strike, it laid him out in bed, shivering violently one moment under layers of blankets, then burning and sweating profusely from a torrid fever the next. It was painful just to see.

III

The Hochstadt House at 14 Parkstone Road

The National Library of Singapore has a number of photos of "The Hochstadt House at 14 Parkstone Road" and one of these has the following annotation: "… photograph shows the Hochstadt House at no. 14 Parkstone Road. The road mentioned is near Tanjong Katong Road and is named after the south of England seaside town. The Hochstadt House is no longer found in the present street directory …".

The Hochstadt House was a large brick and hardwood timber – mainly teak – main building, raised some four-and-a-half feet on brick and cement pillars, for cross ventilation beneath the floor of the main building and to ensure the main building was above the highest flood level, the land there being low-lying and prone to flooding during the northeast monsoon season.

Right up to the 1950s, that property and the area around, like others within that municipal district of Singapore, were not serviced by sewers. The human waste, or night soil, had to be collected regularly – including during the Japanese Occupation – by night soil carriers. They carried two heavy metal buckets each, with lids that could be clipped tightly shut, hung from either end of a wooden pole slung across their shoulders. The buckets were taken to special motor vehicles that had individual compartments, each with a small metal door that could be latched shut. The vehicles would be conveniently parked along the side of nearby roads or streets. When fully loaded, the vehicles would be driven to disposal centres for the buckets to be emptied into large disposal vats.

There had been a disastrous flood in that area of Dunman Estate, which devastated the rubber plantations there, resulting in the land being carved up and sold in lots for new housing. A rich Chinese towkay bought two adjoining plots, 14 Parkstone Road and an adjoining block of vacant land. That vacant land came to be planted with several varieties of fruit trees, including mango, carambola, starfruit, jackfruit, belimbing, sentol, jambu ayer and coconut. There was also a tennis court that was overtaken by a badminton court and, during the Japanese Occupation, beds of tapioca, sweet potato, papaya and sugar cane. After World War II, through disuse and neglect, the land became overgrown with lallang.

The owner of 14 Parkstone Road and the adjoining vacant block, fell on hard times. The entire property was seized by the Municipal Council when they failed to pay their overdue municipal bills for water, electricity and night soil collection. The property was put up for rent by the Municipal Council. My Aunt Nellie and Uncle Fred rented 14 Parkstone Road from the Municipal Council for their family and allowed the use of one room by my father and mother and their two young daughters – Myrna and Cora. I was born in 1933 in a room of that house. Later, my father rented 6 Parkstone Road, which was next to the vacant land adjoining 14 Parkstone Road, from a wealthy Arab landowner when it became vacant and the family of my parents was getting too big to live in just one room.

My younger sister, Joan, was born in a room of 6 Parkstone Road. My three sisters, Myrna, Cora and Joan, were each born in different houses, whereas I and my two brothers, Carl and John, were born in the same room of the same house at 14 Parkstone Road. My parents and family moved back to No. 14 when my Aunt Nellie and Uncle Fred bought 797 Grove – later Mountbatten – Road and moved there with their family. My father continued to rent 14 Parkstone Road from the Municipal Council and live there with his family.

In the late 1940s, the Municipal Council put 14 Parkstone Road and similar properties it had acquired, following default in payment of municipal charges, up for auction. It was bought by another rich Chinese towkay who intended it for his new, young second wife. However, the Rent Control Ordinance, still in force, protected tenants such as my father from eviction. The rich Chinese towkay then built a brand-new house on the adjacent vacant block he owned for his second wife. My father continued to rent No. 14 for he and family to live in, right to his retirement in 1963. He then offered to buy the property with his retirement gratuity, which the landlord accepted. My father continued to live there even after his wife passed away in 1974, and his loyal cook and general factotum, John Baptist, passed away too some years later. My father's children had all married and moved out to live with their own families long before. He lived all alone in that big house, with six bedrooms plus a hall and a living room in the main upper building and another two rooms in servants' quarters in the lower building at ground level. He stayed there right up to his passing on in 1994, aged 86, as he had wished.

My father appointed me administrator of his estate. He willed the property at Parkstone Road to my five siblings in equal shares, leaving me out. He explained that this was because he had willed his entire shareholding in Singapore Casket Co to me, as he did not wish his shareholding in the company to be split amongst several. My siblings agreed to sell the property, which was bought by a developer who demolished all buildings onsite and put up a pair of semi-detached houses instead. Hence that plaintive epitaph alongside the photo of the Hochstadt House on PictureSG, "the Hochstadt House is no longer found in the current street directory"!

I later made a donation to the Eurasian Association, of which I was then patron and trustee, from sale proceeds of my shareholding in Singapore Casket Co when it was bought by an Australian shareholder who wished to acquire 100 per cent of the company. In recognition, the Eurasian Association named the main conference and meeting room in its Eurasian Community House at 139 Ceylon Road, "The John Hochstadt Room" after my paternal grandfather. A marble bust of my grandfather, given to me when Singapore Casket Co was sold, stood on a pedestal at the entrance to that room. A set of framed photos of Grandpa John Hochstadt and Grandma Rosa Delphina and members of the extended family, also hung on a wall inside the room.

IV

Schooldays

During the initial years of the Japanese Occupation, which ran from 1942 to 1945, or 2602 to 2605 by Japanese reckoning, of Singapore or Syonan-to as the Japanese occupiers called it, I attended Ceylon Road Boys' School in the afternoon session of what in pre-occupation days was the St Hilda's School. The morning session at those premises during the occupation was for Ceylon Road Girls' School, which my elder sisters, Myrna and Cora attended, and later my younger sister, Joan, when she came of school-going age. To get to the school, I would walk along Parkstone Road to Tanjong Katong Road towards Grove – later Mountbatten – Road and turn off onto a sandy track through a coconut plantation to Haig Road; from where, I would continue to and along East Coast Road, turning into Marshall Road, then Fowlie Road, and onto Ceylon Road, to school.

A large double-storey timber estate house, raised above ground on timber columns, with an attap roof, stood in the coconut plantation, about three-quarters of the way from Tanjong Katong Road to Haig Road. Sometime toward the end of the occupation, a couple of unserviceable Japanese warplanes were towed under cover of darkness to that coconut plantation and parked under camouflage netting, beneath some tall trees with spreading and leafy branches, near that large double-storey timber estate house in which the manager of the surrounding coconut plantation and his family lived. The aircraft remained there till war's end, when looters got to the aircraft and stripped them bare of all useful or saleable parts and metal and carted away whatever could be salvaged from those aircraft.

A classmate of mine at Ceylon Road Boys' School, was S Suppiah, younger brother of S R Nathan who later became President of the Republic of Singapore. One day during school recess, while in a game of Police & Thieves, I heard a loud, "Psst, psst", coming from outside the thick bougainvillea hedge bordering the school boundary fence along Fowlie Road as I was trying to find a safe place to hide from the police in the game. I peeked through the hedge and saw S R Nathan, who had left Ceylon Boys' School sometime earlier to work as an interpreter for the Japanese to support his mother and younger brother. Nathan signalled to me to crawl through a dry stormwater drain that ran under the hedge to the main stormwater drain that ran along Fowlie Road, which I did. He then beckoned me to follow him along Fowlie Road to Ceylon Road and safe haven within the grounds of the school itself, without getting caught by the police in that game of Police & Thieves.

A classmate in the school who became a good friend was George Netto, who lived with his parents and siblings on Wareham Road, a few roads away from Parkstone Road, between Tanjong Katong and Crescent roads. We often walked home after school together, along Dunman and Tanjong Katong roads to our respective homes. One day, after he had left school to go out to work for a Japanese plant within the boarded-up and fenced-in grounds around the pond where Chung Cheng Chinese High School now stands, he met me as I was walking home from school and invited me to follow him to a stream that ran from the grounds of the Japanese plant, under a barbed-wire fence, to the Geylang River nearby. He asked me to jump into the stream with him to help him catch some small freshwater fish to take to our respective homes for dinner that night. After some time, George ducked under the barbed-wire fence to go into the stream within the grounds of the Japanese plant where he worked and where he said there should be more fish. Just as he did so, an Indian guard who most likely had been hiding behind some nearby bushes ran up to grab George by the wrist for having trespassed into the plant. But George was not at all flustered and very calmly told the guard to release his wrist as he had the permission of the Japanese boss of that plant, and very officiously mentioned his name for good measure. The guard looked most doubtful but probably thought it best to play safe lest he unwittingly antagonised the Japanese boss. He let go of George's wrist and ordered George out of the grounds immediately. George very calmly ducked back under the barbed-wire fence and we both went on our way to our respective homes, with the small catch of fish that we had, most of which George had caught, but which he most graciously volunteered to share equally with me.

A small narrow-gauge railway used to run along Dunman Road, carrying sand from quarries at sand hills around Kaki Bukit. It ran across Tanjong Katong Road and Geylang River to landfills for the old Kallang Airport. While he was still at Ceylon Road Boys' School, George and I would, as the train chugged by with its full load of sand, run along beside the train to try and race it to Tanjong Katong Road. We always beat the train and George usually beat me, except when we tied. George Netto was a great pal and teacher by example in those difficult days of the Japanese Occupation when everything was scarce.

I did not leave Ceylon Road Boys' School, so much as I no longer had a school to go to. Owing to declining attendance due to older boys leaving to go out to work, and to the parents of younger boys who feared their sons might be picked up while on their way to or from school by soldiers and carted off in lorries to be sent to the Siam-Burma Railway to work and very likely die, Ceylon Road Boys' School closed. My father got me transferred to Koon Seng Road School, which occupied the premises of the former Presbyterian Boys' School. It was a single-session, morning-only school for boys, where my father was a teacher. Being a morning-session school, every school day began with Radio Taisho exercises. These were a set of stretching exercises performed to music blaring from the valve radio, to the count of "Ichi, ni, san, shi, goh, roku, sichi, hachi" (One, two, three, four, five, six, seven, eight) repeated over and over again to the end of the set exercises for the day. There was also, every morning, singing of the Japanese national anthem, "Kimigayo", which we had to learn and memorise.

Since the salaries of the teachers, in Japanese "banana notes", were hardly enough for the teachers and their families to live on, especially with the banana notes losing purchasing power day by day, with nothing to back the currency except the "promise to pay", which carried little weight if any, most teachers had little choice but to roster themselves to be away from school regularly so they might, hopefully, be more gainfully engaged at the black market or "Robinson Petang" – Robinsons being the big British-owned department store on Raffles Place in pre-occupation days and *petang* being afternoon in Malay – the black market. So, we schoolboys often had no class teacher and had to make do as best we could ourselves.

There was a classmate of mine at Koon Seng Road School, Brendan James, son of a well-known teacher of Irish extraction,

Frank James, who had been a teacher at St Joseph's Institution in pre-occupation days. Brendan and I got on very well and we started a small vegetable garden on a plot of land in the school compound. We grew sweet potato, yam, chilli, ladies' finger, brinjal and papaya and whatever else would grow there. We took whatever we could harvest, shared equally between us two, home to supplement the meagre food supplies of our families. But there were times when, on getting to school and going to our vegetable plot, we found someone had been there before and raided it, even when the produce was not quite ready for harvesting.

Tales of schoolboys being picked up on the street and shanghaied to work on the dreaded Siam-Burma Railway, led to special identification papers, without photos but with official looking stamps or chops, being issued to each boy in school. The identification papers were to be carried by each schoolboy at all times when out, to be produced if they were stopped in the street by the Japanese. Rumour had it, though, that even boys with such papers might be picked up in the street and sent to work on the railway.

Apart from the period of the Japanese Occupation, when I attended classes at Ceylon Road Boys' School and then Koon Seng Road School, my formal schooling, from Primary 1 to post school certificate, was at St Andrew's School. Before moving to its Graham White Drive location at at Woodsville, St Andrew's School occupied the site at Stamford Road where later a brand-new red brick building for the National Library came up, in the late 1950s. After St Andrew's School moved to Woodsville, a wing of those old school buildings came to house the Corrupt Practices Investigation Bureau from 1962 to 1984. St Andrew's School students, past and present, were wont to proudly proclaim that the school left a good legacy at Stamford Road of literacy and learning in the National

Library, and antipathy to corruption in the Corrupt Practices Investigation Bureau.

Parallel to its location at Stamford Road, but separated by the Stamford Canal running alongside it, was the main playing field of St Joseph's Institution. Beside that playing field ran Bras Basah Road, and across the road, St Joseph's Institution, the premier Roman Catholic boys' school in Singapore. In a prominent position at the front of St Joseph's Institution on a high pedestal, stood a statue of St Jean-Baptiste de la Salle in a flowing robe with right arm raised and outstretched index finger of right hand pointing, seemingly directly to St Andrew's School on Stamford Road. A well-known and much respected principal of St Andrew's School who had served long in that capacity before World War II and after, originally from Adelaide, South Australia, and a Rhodes Scholar graduate of Oxford University, Reverand Canon R K S Adams, used to wickedly jest that the good saint was pointing across Bras Basah Road, the school playing field and Stamford Canal and Road, to St Andrew's School as the best school thereabouts!

My time at St Andrew's School at Stamford Road was short-lived – one term only. My cousin, George Jannings, a couple of years older than I, was already enrolled at St Andrew's when I joined. He was enjoined, by his mother, my Aunt Nellie, to keep an elder brother's eye out for me and make sure I was not bullied. He introduced me to two of his best pals, who were considered to be really tough, Yopie Longpoetieh – minor royalty from Sumatra in the Dutch East Indies – and Gordon White, so they could assist him in his task. Georgie Boy evacuated with his parents and sisters to Perth, Western Australia, at the outbreak of the war. Later, after completing his schooling there, he worked for a bank in Perth where he lived with his family, but died young from a heart attack during a game of squash. Yopie was said to have returned to Sumatra at the outbreak of, or early in, the war. I never heard any more of him. But a relative of Yopie, Donald Longpoetih, was a contemporary of my brother, Carl, at St Andrew's School at Woodsville. Gordon White went on to become a well-known trade unionist in Singapore and later migrated to Australia and I had no more news of him.

The school was to have started operating from the opening of that school year at Woodsville. But owing to delay in construction, the move to Woodsville was deferred to the opening of the second school term instead. My class teacher in Primary 1, at Stamford Road, was Miss Elizabeth Yong – later Mrs Elizabeth Choy – who became a wartime heroine for smuggling scarce supplies to British POWs in the internment camps. She was taken into custody by the Japanese Military Police, or Kempeitai, and tortured, but survived. After the war she was awarded the Order of the British Empire. She was a delight as class teacher. She remembered me into her nineties, as her "good, quiet little boy", which she penned in an autograph for me in a book she wrote in her later years. She continued as my Primary 1 class teacher for some time after the school's move to Woodsville. Miss Mercy Sheares – later Mrs Jansen – younger sister of Benjamin Sheares, one-time Professor of Obstetrics and Gynaecology at the university, who later became President of the Republic of Singapore, was my class teacher in Primary 2 at Woodsville. She was most refreshing as class teacher and a great delight as well! Being still very young, fresh and noticeably shy, the bolder boys in class tended to take advantage of and tease her, which she took in good spirit, while often fiercely blushing.

At the end of the 1941 school year, we in Primary 2, were to be promoted to Standard 1, at secondary level, in the new year of 1942. But World War II intervened. On 15 February 1942, my father's birthday and the first day of the Lunar New Year, Singapore fell to the Japanese Imperial forces of General Tomoyuki Yamashita. The next phase of my schooling, was that interlude of Japanese schools – Ceylon Road Boys' School and Koon Seng Road School – from 1942 to 1945.

When St Andrew's School reopened at Woodsville, following the end of the war, my father took me to a Middle Road shoe store to buy a pair of school shoes – during the occupation years shoes were scarce and expensive and we could only afford sandals with thick rubber soles that tended to melt and stick while we walked along the tarmac heated under the afternoon sun, and thick rubber upper straps that tended to melt and stick to the feet – and thence to St Andrew's School, to get me registered for classes at secondary level. But at the school, they did not really know in which class to put me. There was no objective standard to go by to gauge what level would best suit each student entering or returning to school after the war years. They tended to go by the level they expected each boy to be in, if not for intervention of the war. But there were older boys who had missed out on their schooling during the war years who would have to be fitted in too. It was finally decided I should go into Standard 3.

There I was, in Standard 3 at St Andrew's, when I resumed schooling at the end of the war. But it was by then nearing the end of that school year, and there were no more than a couple of months within which to cram into each student the differing needs of each to make up for what each might have lost out on during the war years. Nevertheless, I must have done relatively well in the year-end examinations, most likely owing to my relative proficiency in the English language. When schools reopened the following year, I was moved two levels up, to Standard 5. That did not turn out too well for me.

The intervention of World War II had caused me to miss out on the traditional Crossing of the Quadrangle, introduced by

Principal Reverend Adams, to denote the ascent from primary to secondary school level in the physical crossing by students from the primary side of that grassy quadrangle, across to the secondary side. Tradition had it that any boy who failed to make that crossing would not be promoted to secondary level at St Andrew's School. But I never did learn of any such actual case. In my double promotion from Standard 3 to 5, I lost out entirely on the basics of elementary mathematics. Resulting in my later having to be specially tutored in mathematics by my Uncle Arthur, my mother's elder brother.

We spoke English at home. And, during the long dreary days at home during the occupation years, with nothing much else safe to do, I voraciously read books from my father's home library, including works of Shakespeare and of other great English writers. My standard of both spoken and written English was, as a result, relatively higher than that of my classmates. I did not suffer any real disadvantage in English language nor subjects which required fluency in the English language on my return to St Andrew's School at the end of the war.

On the last day of my examination for the Cambridge School Certificate, following my final paper in the main hall of St Andrew's School at Woodsville, I was on my way home in a Singapore Traction Company bus. Rounding the corner of High Street and onto St Andrew's Road, I spied a large crowd that had gathered in a procession along the road, before the Supreme Court. They yelled at the bus as it went slowly by and banged their fists against the thin metal side of the bus as it carefully avoided knocking into anyone in the crowd who had spilled towards the centre of the road.

When I got home and was having lunch, I related what had happened to my mother, sisters and brothers, who had already had their lunch and were gathered around the table to listen to what I had to report. I added that the crowd would have gathered there to await the verdict of the court in the Maria Hertogh case. And the crowd appeared to be in an ugly mood. My mother advised my sisters to avoid High Street and the area around the Supreme Court on their intended Christmas shopping that afternoon. The Maria Hertogh case concerned a young Dutch girl who, so her parents claimed, had been left in the custody of a Malay lady just before surrender of Singapore to the Japanese. The Malay lady claimed, in turn, that was not so; Maria had been given to her by the girl's Dutch parents. Furthermore, the Malay lady claimed, Maria had converted from Roman Catholicism to Islam and recently married, under Muslim rites, a young Malay schoolteacher.

My mother further advised my two elder sisters not to take their younger sister, Joan, shopping with them, because Joan looked too much like Maria Hertogh and was about the same age. My mother added that they should avoid going by bus, and take a taxi instead. Myrna and Cora left, taking Carl and John with them. My father got home some time later. The car of my Uncle Fred, driven by my Uncle Fred's Malay driver and with Jimmy Quays, an old and close family friend who lived with my Aunt Nellie and Uncle Fred, on board, pulled into the driveway of our home at 14 Parkstone Road. Jimmy Quays alighted from the car and asked my father to accompany him to my Uncle Fred and Aunt Nellie's home at 797 Mountbatten Road, to telephone my elder sisters, who were then at the YWCA hostel at Canning Rise, with their two younger brothers – there was no telephone at our house then. My father went off in the car with Jimmy Quays. My mother, younger sister, Joan, and I remained at home and were not to see or hear from my father till the next morning. We worried about my father, sisters and brothers through the night, staying glued to the radio news of rioting in Singapore and the imposition of a dusk to dawn curfew.

We later learnt that while Myrna, Cora, Carl and John were on their way to town for their Christmas shopping, their taxi was caught in a traffic jam on Victoria Street. The driver of a taxi coming from the opposite direction, leaned out of his cab when it got abreast of my siblings' taxi and warned them not to go on but turn back, as there was trouble in the city centre. As the road back was jammed, Myrna and Cora told their taxi driver, after a brief consultation between themselves, to take them onward to the YWCA hostel at Canning Rise. A teacher friend of theirs from Penang lodged there and they hoped they could take refuge in the hostel with her help. When they got there, they telephoned my Aunt Nellie to ask that a message be passed to their parents that all four were safe and had taken refuge at the YWCA hostel. But my Aunt Nellie, persuaded by her three anxious but well-meaning grown-up daughters, prevailed upon my father and Jimmy Quays to go in my Uncle Fred's car, driven by the Malay driver, to the YWCA hostel to rescue my siblings.

While my father and Jimmy Quays were travelling along Victoria Street, the car was blocked by a swelling crowd, and could not go on. The Malay driver opened his car door and bolted, never to be seen again by any member of the family. My father and Jimmy Quays were ordered out of the car. As they got out, a leader of the crowd recognised my father, and yelled out, "Cik Gu lama saya", (My old teacher). He ordered the crowd to make way for my father and Jimmy Quays so they could get away from there. My father and Jimmy Quays walked swiftly away. As they left, they saw the car turned on its side and set ablaze. My father and Jimmy Quays found their way on foot to the Municipal Pig Abattoir nearby, where Jimmy Quays was a superintending health inspector and declared they should be safe there at the pig abattoir from any rioting. They spent the night there. Next morning, when the curfew was lifted, they walked to nearby Singapore Casket Co on Lavender Street and got a lift from a company car and driver there to their respective homes.

Later that morning, Myrna, Cora, Carl and John, were delivered home, safe and sound, in a British military Land Rover under armed British military escort. It was specially arranged by a fellow YWCA lodger of their good friend, who took pity on them and personally arranged it through an officer friend at the British military garrison. Myrna and Cora had earlier been ordered by the officious English lady superintendent of the YWCA hostel to take their two young brothers and leave the hotel because males were not permitted on the premises. When my sisters' friend remonstrated that the two boys were still very young, not even in their teens, and it would not be safe yet for them and their two elder sisters to venture through an area that had seen street riots the previous night, without any police escort, the English lady hostel superintendent haughtily told my sisters to arrange whatever police escort they needed themselves. But when my sisters telephoned the police officer on duty at a designated call centre, the British officer in charge bluntly told them armed escorts were only for "Europeans" and refused to budge.

***

Between the entrance examination for entry to the University of Malaya and opening of the new academic year, while I was employed as a temporary clerk at the Teachers' Training College at its premises at Cairnhill Road, I enlisted in the Malayan Royal Naval Volunteer Reserve (MRNVR), with its headquarters on HMS *Laburnum*, an ex-Japanese navy minesweeper minus any engine that was permanently moored alongside the quay at Telok Ayer Basin. I asked to be enrolled in a technical branch and was enlisted as an electrician rating. Being Eurasian, and therefore deemed to be "other than European" under the British colonial classification of the time, I could not have been appointed a commissioned officer in any non-technical branch. As an electrician rating, I had to attend evening classes twice a week at the Balestier Road Trade School, to get a London City & Guilds electrician certification. But, after a year at that and with most of those enlisting with me dropping out, those classes came to an end and I dropped out too from the MRNVR.

On the introduction of limited National Service in Singapore in 1954 – as a result of which there was trouble on the streets following demonstrations by Chinese middle school students who objected to national service under British colonialists and even rioted – I returned to the MRNVR to volunteer, rather than enlist in National Service. I requested transfer to the Executive Branch, which was granted, and I was signed on in the rank of probationary acting sub-lieutenant. The policy had changed by then in the lead up to Malayan independence in 1957 and Singapore statehood in 1959, to allow other than Europeans to be taken on as officers in the Executive Branch. In that capacity I was required to undergo a minimum of two weeks' sea training a year. I did so aboard the MRNVR's specially designed and built HMS *Panglima*. It was built at the Thornycroft Shipyard, at its slipway at Tanjong Rhu. I attended the launching ceremony of HMS *Panglima*, a grand affair with champagne flowing, at that slipway.

My first, two weeks' sea training, aboard HMS *Panglima*, was to Langkawi, Penang and Telok Anson, now Telok Intan, up the Perak River, under command of Commander Fleming, retired Royal Navy, who was employed as staff officer at HMS *Laburnam*. The Suez War was just on then and there were rumours the *Panglima* might be ordered to the Suez. It was an interesting, though uneventful, voyage. At a reception aboard the vessel at Langkawi for local dignitaries, especially of the resident British elite, the Malay District Medical Officer of the area who was a graduate of the medical college in the grounds of the Singapore General Hospital and part of the University of Malaya, had been invited but failed to make an appearance. He was said to have failed to do so for political reasons. Malaya was then on the cusp of independence, which it got in 1957, and the United Malays National Organisation (UMNO) was flexing its muscles.

The following year I went on a two-week sea training voyage again aboard HMS *Panglima* to Kuching and then up the Rejang River to Sibu, Sarawak. The voyage to Kuching was stormy, with the northeast monsoon blowing across the South China Sea. On the voyage to Kuching, while going down the ladder from the deck to the toilet in the wardroom, where the officers' bunks, dining table, shower and toilet were, a big wave struck the vessel head-on as I stepped off the bottom rung of the ladder and sent me sprawling headfirst against the edge of the dining table. I split my forehead open and the cut bled profusely. There was no doctor on board nor even any medical orderly, so I had to clean and dress the wound myself, as best I could, using a first aid kit. I carried that dressing, with wound beneath, to Sibu and back to Telok Ayer Basin and home.

We took a pilot on board going upriver to Kuching. He was a wiry and garrulous man, from Liverpool, I later discovered, from whence my maternal grandfather Captain John Phillips originated. He was in his early fifties, I guessed, and very friendly, to me at least though I did sense members of his local expatriate community of public officers seemed rather cool towards him. I was later to discover why. At the reception on board HMS *Panglima* that evening he got talking to me, mainly, I felt, because few others there seemed to want to talk or even be polite to him. He invited me to his home, a little further upriver from where our vessel was tied alongside the dock, for lunch the next day and told me he would seek permission for me from HMS *Panglima*'s commanding officer (CO) should I agree and he would send a Land Rover to pick me up from our vessel and send me back after. I readily agreed and he promptly sought and got permission from my CO. Next day I discovered the pilot's English wife had passed away from some illness years before, leaving him and their young son to both – as the snobs in his community of expat public officers in Sarawak snootily complained – "go native"; the pilot took to cohabiting with his three chosen Dyak companions from longhouses of the immediate surrounds in Kuching. During the lunch at the pilot's home I did see three very attractive young Dyak women, seated cross-legged on a mat on the floor of the room in which the pilot and I ate our meal. The Dyak women would, from time to time, get up in turn to serve us dishes for our lunch and clear away empties, while constantly administering most attentively to our drink and miscellaneous luncheon needs. A fair but very tanned young lad with flowing blond hair, wearing only white shorts, suddenly appeared through the trees lining the sides of the mud path that led up from the river to the house. He came bounding up the path, while the pilot and I were still lunching, and yelled with a wide grin and flashing white teeth, "Kapal perang, kapal perang!" (Warship, warship!), pointing down to the river then bounding off along another path to have a better look at HMS *Panglima*. He was soon lost to our sight. The pilot turned to look at me and, with a gentle and very indulgent broad smile, said proudly, "My son thinks he's something out of Joseph Conrad!"

***

While at Kuching some of the officers on board, including me and our chief petty officer were driven in two Land Rovers on a visit to a large and well-maintained longhouse about forty-five minutes away along a mud road through the jungle. There we were seated cross-legged on a large mat on the timber floor of the veranda while some half dozen young Dyak women of the longhouse went round to each of us in turn to serve us from a large earthenware jug filled with *tuak*, the Dyak speciality rice wine. A woman carrying a jug of *tuak* would pour some of the contents of the jug into the large earthenware mug held by another young Dyak woman until the mug was brimful and flowing over. The brimful mug would then be held to the open mouth of each guest in turn and the *tuak* poured down his throat. Should any guest not be able to gulp down the whole mug of *tuak* at one go or be fast enough to satisfy his mug-wielding maiden, she would pour the remaining *tuak* over the guest's head, letting the liquor flow down over his shoulders and onto his shirt, to the noisy glee of all. Knowing how the *tuak* was made did not help it go down any easier. On the drive to the longhouse we had been told by a local officer, who had been assigned to accompany us, that on a prescribed day the young Dyak women chewed raw grains of rice from a stock in a basket nearby, then spat out the masticated grains, liberally lubricated with their saliva, into a large earthenware jar. The jar would then be covered and stored in a dark and cool corner of the longhouse, for the enzymes in the well-masticated grains to do their job of fermentation – miraculously turning the rice grains into the invigorating and intoxicating *tuak*!

***

While HMS *Panglima* was berthed alongside the Rejang River at Sibu, I found that the reception on board the ship would be attended by Dr Xavier, a doctor qualified at the King Edward VII College of

Medicine in Singapore, who had married Flora Kechil, daughter of Aunt Annie, and set up practice in Sibu, where he had settled down before World War II. He became a prominent and respected member of the Sibu community, no doubt partly because he was the only doctor there. He was reported to be often recompensed for medical services rendered and medication provided by way of live chickens or ducks and baskets of their eggs, or the occasional live goat or pig, or with local fruit or vegetables instead of cash, which was scarce in that location. Dr Xavier had not been pre-warned I would be in the complement of HMS *Panglima*. When he came aboard for the reception and after he had extended his greetings to the CO and other senior officers, I went up to welcome him and introduce myself. He was very pleasantly surprised and told me then and there that I had to go back with him to his home nearby in Sibu and say hello to his wife, my cousin Flora Kechil, and their family and have a home-cooked dinner of some delectable local dishes. So at the reception's close I sought permission from the CO to leave with Dr Xavier to visit my cousin and her family, and promptly left with Dr Xavier in his car for his home. Flora Kechil was most surprised to see me but very pleasantly so. She got a delicious dinner served up for Dr Xavier and me while Dr Xavier took out a bottle of his best whisky to get glass after glass of "whisky stengah" served to us at the dining table by his young male servant or "Boy". After our dinner we sat in Dr Xavier's comfortable living room overlooking his large front garden planted with a variety of local fruit trees. Around midnight Dr Xavier said it was too late for me to return to the vessel and asked Flora Kechil to show me to their spare guest room. I was given a fresh sarong to change into after a shower and a promise that I would be woken first thing in the morning. Dr Xavier woke me promptly early the next morning and, after a quick morning wash and change, followed by a hearty breakfast of ham and two fried eggs sunny side up, plus toast and copious mugs of sugarless black coffee, Dr Xavier's driver returned me to HMS *Panglima* in the doctor's car. I climbed the gangway and onto the quarterdeck, saluted and greeted the CO who stood there and saluted and greeted me back with nary a word nor smile nor any look of admonishment for failing to return to the ship the previous night. But later I was ordered to present myself to the bridge where the CO admonished me soundly for failing to return to ship the previous night, as I should have.

V

University Days

I did not really get involved in student activities in my earlier years at university, mainly because I was going steady with a fellow young undergraduate. She was from Taiping, Malaya, where her father was a schoolteacher, and she initially stayed in the university hostel for ladies at Mount Rosie during term. After she was admitted to the university, her father got a transfer to a Catholic mission-aided school in Singapore and moved with his wife and whole family, comprising my girlfriend's five younger siblings – four sisters and a brother – to live with him in Singapore. Her father, mother and siblings initially stayed at her maternal grandfather's home on Branksome Road, just roads away from Parkstone, before moving to their own rental apartment on East Coast Road, a short ten-minute motorcycle ride from my home at 14 Parkstone Road. I gave her lifts on my motorcycle, from Mount Rosie to her family home and back on the weekends, and during the week in term, on request, as and when. We also often went for evening and weekend rides around Singapore and sometimes even across the Causeway to Johore, Malaya, to take the air or *makan angin*, for shopping, to the cinema and for lunch or dinner. We were very close and spent much time together. Our fellow students predicted we would marry on graduation. But we broke up in the final year of my BA (Pass) degree, which left me with a deep sense of loss for that constant companionship, and concern as to how to fill the time that then hung heavy. Around that time too, I had a young German mathematics lecturer, whose lectures often left me, and others too, at a complete loss! Which in turn led to loss of interest in whatever he taught and a growing despondency. Skipping his lectures left even more time on my hands. I spent much time then in the university library reading books on the "Theory of Numbers", which for some reason fascinated me at the time, and also on periodicals and books in philosophy, which I found much to my liking and interest. I also spent time at the cinema with Joe Conceicao, a mature student who had qualified as a normal trained teacher and subsequently taught at St Patrick's School. He was at the university on a teaching bursary, in what was referred to as the "Honeymoon Year" during which there were no examinations and he could spare the time indulging his passion for the cinema. He lived at Karikul Lane, not far from my home at 14 Parkstone Road. Besides often giving him a lift home from the university, I often gave him a lift from the university to the cinema and then home. That gave him an added incentive to invite me to go to the cinema with him, which I only too readily accepted. Owing to a combination of all that, and more, I failed my final BA (Pass) degree and had to repeat.

Failing is not necessarily a bad thing and can be good, if one learns from it. I most probably did. We had to take two subjects at principal level then and one at subsidiary for the BA (Pass) degree. I took English literature and pure mathematics at principal level in my repeat year, as I had the previous year, and philosophy at subsidiary level. I had earlier sat in as a non-graduating student on lectures in philosophy and found the latter very interesting, so asked to be allowed to take philosophy at subsidiary level for my repeat BA (Pass), as well as make it the subject of specialisation for my BA (Honours) degree. Special approval was granted on the recommendation of the Head of the Department of Philosophy, Dr John Hartland-Swann, with the support and approval of Professor Alexander Oppenheim, then Dean of the Faculty and Professor of Mathematics. Perhaps Professor Oppenheim just wanted troublesome me out his Mathematics Department and hair, which was already white then.

I was told that, coincidentally, the combination of English literature and pure mathematics at principal level, and philosophy, at subsidiary, was not repeated following my doing so by any other student at the university until Angelina (or Angel) Phillips, eldest daughter of my late cousin, Jackie Phillips, did so years later. The special approval granted me was conditional on my sitting in on philosophy lectures at principal level for the second and third years of the BA (Pass), so that I might catch up on what I had not covered. I passed the BA (General) in that repeat year with English literature and pure mathematics at principal level and philosophy at subsidiary. The next year I went on to do my BA (Honours) in philosophy and obtained second-class honours, upper division.

It was only in my BA (Pass) repeat year that I took any serious interest in and began to get actively involved in student affairs. Thanks mainly to my fellow undergraduate, Henry Chia, who introduced me to a bunch of undergraduates, junior to both of us, who were easy-going but intellectual and prone to serious discussions, especially after a few beers. An interesting American lecturer in philosophy, Frank Cioffi, who buried his face in a book while walking from the university along Nassim Road to Orchard Road, used to say he wished he could serve beer to his students during tutorials to get the discussions really going. That bunch were unconventional and great fun to be with. Henry Chia and the others – Sarjit Singh, Ernest Wong, Haider Sithawalla and Ho Wah Kam – became among my best friends at university and even after. We had great times together. But Henry Chia and Ho Wah Kam later dropped out of that group.

Though not in that group, my other close friends at the time included the late Lloyd Fernando, who became a professor in the Department of English in the University of Malaya in Kuala Lumpur, and then went on to be called to the Bar and practiced as a lawyer in Kuala Lumpur; Joe Conceicao, my fellow film buff, who became an academic at the university and an MP in the Singapore Parliament, and then Ambassador for the Republic of Singapore to several countries; and Charles Keel, who after graduation worked for a British trading house, then for a time in the Singapore Ministry of Interior & Defence, and later returned to the UK where his parents were from originally and to which they had returned. Later, Ratna Lolan, from Malacca, and very much my junior at university, often referred to as "Socialist", became a great friend too. He did not finish university in Singapore and graduate from the University of Malaya. Some close friends, led by Sarjit Singh, got a collection going from amongst us former fellow students so Ratna Lolan could go by ship to an Italian port and from there overland to London to do his Bar exams. But he died there some years later without qualifying as a lawyer.

In the long university vacation at the end of my first year, I took on a job at Singapore Casket Co to earn some spending money. It entailed attending and overseeing funerals. With earnings from that, I bought a second-hand Triumph Tiger 100 500cc twin-cylinder motorbike from Bruce MacRae Smith, a Britisher employed by a British trading house off Raffles Place who was a keen motorsports fan and had modified the bike for events organised by the Singapore Motor Club. I had learned to ride a motorbike when my father purchased a new Morris Minor and traded his old Morris Eight Tourer – which he had inherited second-hand from Singapore Casket Co when the latter acquired a new Ford Prefect as the company's general workhorse – for a Triumph 3HW 350cc single-cylinder motorbike owned by Chong Ah Wah, a fellow teacher of my father's at Geylang English school, for me to use to go to and from my post school certificate classes at St Andrew's School. This trade was conditional on Chong Ah Wah personally teaching me to ride and ensuring I got my driving licence, which I did at the first go. I later sold my Triumph 3HW to Maurice Carroll, a managerial assistant at Singapore Casket Co, who came from Miri in Sarawak and was a nephew of my Uncle Carlo Webb, then MD of Singapore Casket Co.

It was Maurice Carroll who told me about my Grand-Uncle Charlie's handsome and muscular son in Miri from his Iban consort when Charles Hochstadt, my grand-uncle, was lighthouse keeper off Miri. Maurice shared this story as he and I were enjoying a leisurely Tiger Beer at the rooftop beer garden of the White House Hotel on Jalan Besar, where Maurice and I used often to adjourn to relax over a beer or two after a day's work at Singapore Casket Co.

***

During the long vacation at the end of my BA (Pass) repeat year, I joined a team from the University of Malaya Archaeological Society on an excavation expedition to Kota Kuala Muda in Kedah, Malaya. Charles Keel and another fellow student who owned and rode a motorbike, Chen Men Sheng, and I rode there and back on our motorbikes. Henry Chia had intended to ride pillion on my bike there and back. But I decided, just before setting off for Kota Kuala Muda, that I had best give my by then not-so-young Triumph Tiger 100 a thorough check and overhaul, including the replacement of any necessary parts. Before embarking on that long journey from Singapore, at the southern tip of Malaya, to Kota Kuala Muda, at the northwest end of Malaya, not too far from the Malayan border with Thailand. I knew how to service my motorcycle and had done so before. But on that occasion, I found a part in the gearbox had best be replaced but could not find such part at any of my regular motorcycle parts vendors in Singapore. So I had to place an order for the part with my regular vendor who assured me he would get the replacement part for me within a day. Convinced that I could not get my bike ready and fit to leave as planned for that long ride to Kota Kuala Muda and back, I advised the others by phone through Henry Chia to go ahead first without me, with Henry Chia riding pillion on Charles Keel's bike. Off they went, agreeing to meet me at a set time a couple of days later at Prai Railway Station in Butterworth.

The following day, after I had got and replaced the part and was feeling confident my bike was ready for that long ride, I left alone on my Triumph Tiger 100, a little too late to make it all the way to Prai in one go. I rode instead to Seremban and stopped overnight at a small lodging house over a corner coffee shop along the main thoroughfare through Seremban. The next morning, after a good sleep and rest in that small lodging house, followed by a hearty breakfast of two half-boiled eggs with buttered toast and a cup of steaming black coffee, or kopi-o, in the corner coffee shop, I got on my bike and rode up and through Mantin Pass and on, all the way with no trouble to Prai Railway Station, arriving in good time for my rendezvous with Charles Keel, Chen Men Sheng and Henry Chia. Henry Chia then switched to ride pillion on my bike and off we set for the designated assembly point in Kota Kuala Muda.

The assembly point was a former rest house set up during British rule in Malaya for British officers of the administration who needed a place to stopover for a couple of days or so when on their rounds of the district; travel overland in those days being not too easy nor speedy. But as the British administration wound down in the lead up to Malayan independence in 1957, the need for such rest houses became less and less. That particular rest house had been disused for some time and was closed. On an earlier recce to the area by K G Tregonning – not yet Raffles Professor of History – and his small team of students from the Department of History of the University of Malaya, that disused rest house had been identified as a base for the excavation team to work from. Arrangements had been made with local authorities for the rest house to be opened, cleaned and spruced up, to serve as the operating base. Dr H A Lamb and Dr C M Turnbull, lecturers in the History Department who were leading the excavation team, had driven from Singapore with a few members of the team in a large Austin car that used to serve as an official vehicle for the university's vice chancellor. The rest of the team were to meet them at that former rest house in Kota Kuala Muda.

The two team leaders, Dr Lamb and Dr Turnbull, were to sleep in two separate rooms at the old rest house, while another large room was to serve as the place for the student excavators to sleep in, on the floor, and the big hall was to serve as the main indoor workroom and dining hall for the team. Some local objection was voiced, however, to male and female team members sleeping in the same room, even though it was large and the two teams of male and female would be sleeping separate and quite far apart. So, the male student members of the team were offered a place to sleep in a large spare room on the upper floor of the local kathi's home, that was usually used by locals from surrounding villages on their way to pilgrimage to Mecca and which the kathi had kindly agreed to loan for male members of our team to sleep in. Among the female team members from

Singapore were Leong Sow Ling, and Ranu Bhattarcharya, plus the all-girl terrible team of Harender Kaur, Rosina Monteiro and Helen Deborah from which I managed to get the approbation before the whole archaeological team dispersed following the dig that "You're not such a bad guy after all." The room the male students were asked to sleep in was at the back of the kathi's house, on the upper level, with a separate back entrance down a flight of wooden stairs. A short way from the bottom of those stairs was a bathroom, with wooden plank walls, and a fresh water well at the centre. We male student team members enjoyed having communal baths there on return from each day's hard dig, singing and joking while drawing clear and refreshingly cold water from the well in pails at the end of long ropes to throw over ourselves and bathe with.

All the team members were initially deployed on a low-lying site off the main highway where remains of what might once have been a small wooden temple on stone foundations were uncovered. While the rest of the team continued to work that site, some in the team, comprising Charles Keel, Chen Men Sheng, Henry Chia and I – probably because we had own transport via our bikes – were deployed to explore a rubber holding some distance away off the main highway. We had to ride along the raised mud bunds between the paddy fields, which served to divide the paddy fields into smaller individual plots. The bunds also served the locals as their own motorcycle, bicycle or pedestrian byways to and from their homes, rubber holdings and paddy fields. The earlier recce team had been told by the locals of some buried artefact or artefacts, including sandstone carvings, there. Indeed, a sandstone block on which was carved a bas relief figure of the Hindu elephant god, Ganesh, whose face had been chipped away in the period of early Islamic fervour, was unearthed there. It was the prize find of that whole excavation expedition.

The same team was then deployed on Bukit Batu Lintang, or Split Stone Hill, a hillock off the main highway. The split stone was in fact a square sandstone base with a square hole in the centre, said to have been where the foot of a stone lingam, or phallus, once stood. But the lingam was long since gone, stolen or destroyed. Though if destroyed, no remnants of any stone lingam did we find. But in the ground around that sandstone base, several pottery and porcelain shards were unearthed. Most interesting of the finds there were bits of broken gold jewellery. These had to be kept a close secret, less the suspicion of villagers and their friends from elsewhere who were always hanging around, was confirmed that our team was really out looking for treasure, and would tear our excavation sites apart looking for treasure of their own. Some in the team postulated the jewellery might well have once belonged to members of the harem of the legendry Rajah Bersiong, or "King with Tusks", whose territory was said to have been in that area.

That whole experience was very enlightening and interesting. There were some good finds, especially that damaged bas-relief carving of Ganesh. All were officially documented, and some put on display in the University of Malaya Arts Museum in Singapore, then under art historian Dr Michael Sullivan. Later, the Arts Museum ceased to exist when most of its collection, including those finds from our dig at Kota Kuala Muda, were transferred to a museum in Kuala Lumpur. Unfortunately those finds were then just stored there and never put on display.

Following that expedition to Kota Kuala Muda, I was elected vice president of the University of Malaya Archaeological Society, at its annual general meeting (AGM) the following year. In that capacity I was tasked to lead a dig for the society in a rear courtyard of the old red Dutch Stadthuys in Malacca. No lecturers from the History Department were there to oversee and supervise the dig.

Instead, a very recent history graduate, Christopher Hooi, who had been President of the University of Malaya Archaeological Society in his student days and was then assistant curator at the Raffles Museum, later the National Museum of Singapore, was allowed by his curator boss, Dr C A Gibson-Hill, to serve as adviser and leader to oversee and supervise the dig. The whole team stayed at the Methodist Boys' School, which was in vacation at the time. One dormitory block served as the home for the boys, including Christopher Hooi, and another, for the girls. Nothing of note or of any great interest was unearthed or discovered there. But my "socialist" friend from university, Ratna Lolan from Malacca, who was then home during the long university vacation, introduced me to his much senior in age Chinese "Socialist Uncle", also from Malacca. He, Ratna Lolan and I, spent many a long evening dining on steamboats and drinking bottles of Bulldog, or Guinness, stout and Tiger Beer, all at the expense of Ratna Lolan's Socialist Uncle. While having endless discussions on politics and socialism and the future of an independent Malaya and an uncertain Singapore. We always met at the Socialist Uncle's favourite restaurant, a corner shophouse unit on the main Malacca thoroughfare of Jalan Bunga Raya, or Hibiscus Lane.

The following year at university, I was elected to the Students' Council of the University of Malaya. In that capacity, I was actively involved, with my good friends and fellow student councillors, Sarjit Singh, Haider Sithawalla and Ernest Wong, in several student activities, and was appointed through the machinations of Ratna Lolan as chairman of the Fundraising Committee for the Algerian Students' Relief Fund. Through the offices of and persuasion by Ratna Lolan, I was also elected to the Central Working Committee of the University of Malaya Socialist Club, as publications secretary. I had shortly before been cleared by the Special Branch to be co-editor with Lloyd Fernando of a publication, *Write*, jointly founded by Lloyd and me, which appeared only as and when, at no fixed interval, and died after just a few issues. It was hoped, having been cleared to co-publish *Write*, I might similarly be able to get *Fajar* going again. But it was not to be. *Fajar* had been banned and proscribed and was not allowed to resume publication. Till the following year, after my tenure as publications secretary of the University of Malaya Socialist Club had ended, and when my good friend, Gopinath Pillai, was elected publications secretary of the University of Malaya Socialist Club.

I was entrusted to bring out, on behalf of the Raffles Society, a published collection of short stories by students past and current of the university. It was *The Compact*. Raffles Society was a society of the University of Malaya for matters of general literary and cultural interest. At one time, before Malaya gained independence in 1957, some student members of the society came up with the idea of EngMalChin, a common language for the independent Malaya comprising a mix of English, Malay, Chinese and Indian languages – Indian being represented by the "in" within "Chinese". But it never took off. As might be expected. I was also enlisted to help set up the University of Malaya Drama Society, hived off from the earlier University of Malaya Debating and Drama Society. In that role I discovered a hitherto unrealised flair in drafting when helping to draft a constitution for the new society.

There was on that drafting committee a wise fellow student who was au fait with politics and political institutions. From him, in discussions while drafting the constitution for the new University of Malaya Drama Society, I learnt about politics in general and political institutions such as the American collegiate electoral system. I learnt a lot then. All in all, I led a very active extracurricular student life in my latter student years of university.

Lim Soon Chye, Ho Wing Meng, Lloyd Fernando and I were the first BA (Honours) graduates in philosophy of the University of Malaya. One of our lecturers told Lloyd and me, in confidence, that all four had done well in the final examination and, in his opinion, merited being awarded first class honours, and that the external examiner was that way inclined too. However, as it was the first time honours in philosophy were being awarded, it would not do, nor would the faculty agree, for all four candidates to get first class honours. So only one, Lim Soon Chye, got first class. The rest of us got second class, upper division.

Lim Soon Chye had been expected to be the most likely to go on to do his master's, then a PhD, and become an academic. But he did not. Lloyd Fernando had been in the university on a teaching bursary and was expected by the Ministry of Education, which awarded the bursary, to do his BA (Honours) degree in English literature, which he had taken at principal level for his BA (Pass) – English literature being a teaching subject, or one taught in schools, while philosophy was not. But he took philosophy instead. He just did so, without asking permission or notifying the Ministry of Education. By the time the Ministry got to know, he was well into the honours course in philosophy. While arguing and bargaining with the Ministry, he continued with the philosophy course, completed it and sat for the final examination. He then went on to do his BA (Honours) in English literature at the university. Following that, he lectured in English literature at the University of Malaya in Kuala Lumpur. Ho Wing Meng and I both opted for the master's degree course in philosophy at the university.

The master's course was a dissertation-only programme. My dissertation supervisor was initially Dr Russi F Khan, a Parsi from Bombay. He had got his PhD from London University. It soon became clear that the topic I had elected to research for my master's would not provide adequate material for any acceptable dissertation. So, I applied for permission to change my topic, which was granted. But as the new topic would fall more under the ambit of Dr Eugene Kamenka's expertise, he became my new supervisor.

I had been appointed a graduate assistant – which paid a monthly stipend of $400, quite princely in those days for a fresh graduate with no experience. As graduate assistant, I was required to spend a specified number of hours each week on tutorials with students. My tutorials happened to be with first-year law students on formal logic. The tutorials were in the evenings. The recently established Law Faculty had introduced evening classes to cater to both full-time and part-time law students, so that those in full-time employment who had not had the opportunity to study law but would like to, could do so and qualify as lawyers, though over an extended period of part-time study.

At my first tutorial with those first-year law students, I told them I did not see the need for students of the law to study formal logic nor for me to tutor them in it. But since I was paid to do so, and they were required to study it for their law course, we had best get on with it as well as we could. I thought the best way for me to do so would be to set exercises in logical argument, and so I did. Several in that tutorial class of thirty to forty students became successful lawyers. One, S Rajendran, became a good friend of mine and a judge of the Supreme Court of Singapore.

My good friend, Henry Chia, who had graduated with BA (Honours) at the same time as I, applied on graduation to join the Singapore Administrative Service. He was selected by the Public Service Commission (PSC) and joined the service. The following year, when my good friends Sarjit Singh, Ernest Wong and Haider Sithawalla graduated with their BA (Honours) in economics, Sarjit Singh persuaded me to apply with him and his fellow economics graduate, Ngiam Tong Dow, to the PSC for the Singapore Administrative Service as well. Ernest Wong, who had been on a teaching bursary, applied for and was awarded a Rotary Fellowship by the Rotary Club of Singapore to go to the University of British Columbia in Vancouver, Canada, for his master's degree. Haider Sithawalla, who had also been on a teaching bursary, initially opted out of teaching to take up a job in the Statistics Department. Later he was amongst the first to take up employment as a senior officer in the newly established Economic Develoment Board (EDB). Sarjit Singh, Ngiam Tong Dow and I were all selected for the Singapore Administrative Service.

Sarjit Singh and Ngiam Tong Dow both accepted their offers and took up appointment soon after the general election of 1959, following the election of the People's Action Party (PAP) to government on 31 May. I was still in the university then, as a graduate assistant in the Department of Philosophy working towards my master's, so I did not take up the offer. I had, in fact, applied for the service with Sarjit Singh and Ngiam Tong Dow, on their persuasion, more as a possibility in reserve in case of need.

***

Peggy Leong Wai Chee, who later became my wife, was in the same BA (Honours) year as Sarjit Singh, Ernest Wong and Haider Sithawalla and was a good friend of theirs. She often took some of them, and me too, out in her small 500cc Fiat Marvelette car for evening rides or for a meal or to the cinema. During a university vacation, she and her good friend, Pat Stephens, drove in her car, accompanying Sarjit Singh in his Austin A30 with Ernest Wong and I along, to Mersing for a short break at that Malayan east coast resort. When we got to Mersing, we found the rest house where we had intended to stay booked out except for one room, which

Sarjit, Ernest and I agreed to offer to Peggy and Pat, while we three young men stayed in one room in a small Chinese-owned hotel nearby.

After checking and settling in, we walked to the nearby beach for a swim though the tide was out. Having waded out for some distance and finding the water was still only about waist deep, I plunged in on a shallow dive, hoping to be able to glide into deeper water and swim. But I struck a small reef just below the water surface, resulting in a cut on the bridge of my nose and much bleeding. We were advised to get it attended to at a nearby clinic, else the wound might get septic. The others dashed with me to a nearby clinic where an Indian dresser cleaned and stitched the wound and dressed it. There were no antibiotics in the clinic and, as I am allergic to anti-tetanus serum, the dresser advised I get the wound attended to by a doctor as soon as possible and get an antibiotic shot as well. Since it was felt by all in our party that it would be best to get that done back in Singapore, and it was too late to do so that evening, we left Mersing early the next morning. When we got to Singapore that evening I consulted my doctor who gave me an antibiotic shot and commended the Indian dresser for having done an excellent job in stitching up the wound. He added that such hospital assistants, or dressers, were often better than doctors in the treatment of minor wounds and illnesses.

Peggy Leong Wai Chee did her BA (Honours) in philosophy the year after I did mine. She also got a second class, upper division. After which she went on to get a Diploma in Education in preparation for a career in teaching, which she never really undertook, instead joining the University Library as probationary assistant librarian. Our American philosophy lecturer, Frank Cioffi, remarked once while she was undergoing her BA (Honours) philosophy course that she was intelligent but "a lazy cow", who had not taken the time to read up and prepare before his tutorial. But when he saw her soon after in a difficult leading role of a university drama society play, he remarked that if she had spent her time preparing and rehearsing for that role, rather than preparing and reading up for his tutorial, she could be forgiven. Such was her performance! She was a keen player in amateur dramatics and starred in several leading roles to much acclaim and often had long discussions with my father, who had been keen on and participated in amateur dramatics in the Singapore Teachers' Union drama section. She also was, and had been for some years already, a popular part-time newsreader on radio. Later, following graduation from the university, she joined the university library and rose, over time, to become its one and only chief librarian, before that post reverted to librarian.

Peggy was the daughter of the third wife of a rich Chinese merchant, who had a big two-storey house on Tanglin Road, a prime residential area of Singapore and an enclave of the rich British expatriate community and wealthy or well-connected local Chinese. He had four wives. Peggy's mother, Yeow Yoke Lan, being the third. In the late 1930s after the Japanese occupied Manchuria, or Manchuko, contributions were collected from amongst the Chinese of Singapore to support those in China fighting the Japanese. Peggy's father was a contributor to the China Relief Fund. When the Japanese occupied Singapore during World War II, an informer identified him as a contributor. He was taken into custody by the Kempeitai, or Japanese Military Police, and severely tortured. He succumbed to the torture and perished in custody. Peggy's mother took her children then to a Buddhist temple for refuge for the rest of the occupation. She swore at that time that if they got through the war alive and well, she would become a Buddhist nun after Peggy, her younger child, was married. Which she did. But in the interim between war's end and Peggy's marriage to me, she ran separate vegetarian restaurants at various times, catering mainly to Buddhists who were vegetarians. She had become a good cook of vegetarian dishes while in refuge at the Buddhist temple and later even had a book of her vegetarian recipes published . She was a very intelligent and most enterprising lady.

***

Following the general election of 1959, the new PAP government declared it was duty-bound to go on an austerity drive. They proclaimed the kitty was bare and government expenditure had to be trimmed and salaries for senior civil servants cut. Talk was rampant of budget cuts for and in the university as well. It was rumoured that since philosophy was considered not essential nor even important – unlike science and engineering – it was a most likely target for budget cuts. Continuance of my graduate assistantship, hence, seemed in doubt.

I conferred with my good friend Sarjit Singh, who by then was already in the Establishment Division of the Ministry of Finance. He advised it might be best for me to take up the offer of appointment in the Administrative Service and for him to do some sounding out of the possibility with the Establishment Division, which was responsible for all civil service appointments in the government. He soon got back to me that, in normal circumstances an offer for appointment to the Administrative Service which was not accepted in good time would, even if not actually rejected, be deemed to have lapsed. However, in view of several resignations from the service following the general election and the salary cuts for senior officers, I could be taken into the Administrative Service. Should I formally accept the offer that had been extended to me.

VI

Working Life: The Early Years

So, there I was, in the Singapore Administrative Service, in November 1959. Sarjit Singh and Ngiam Tong Dow were already there some months earlier. My first appointment was to the Establishment Division of the Ministry of Finance, which was then in the government offices at Empress Place. Tan Chok Kian was my immediate boss and Oon Khye Kiang, the Permanent Secretary. Dr Goh Keng Swee was Finance Minister, with an office in the Fullerton Building, to where the whole Finance Ministry, including the Establishment Division, was relocated not too long after I started.

My boss at the Establishment Division of Finance Ministry, Tan Chok Kian, delegated several interesting projects to me. In the run up to the general election of 1959, it had been declared that the City Council would be dismantled and its functions integrated into the government. One of the two last remaining British expatriate officers in the Singapore Civil Service, A G B (Tony) Colton, a Deputy Secretary in the Establishment Division and due to leave the service shortly under the Malayanisation programme, had amongst his other duties and responsibilities, been entrusted with integration into the government of the daily-rated employees of the former City Council, who numbered several thousand. They were noted for their militant union, led by K Suppiah. My boss, Tan Chok Kian, told me to pick up the work Colton had already done on this over the past several months and nearing completion so as to be able to take over from Colton as soon as I could and help implement the whole integration plan.

I asked Colton to give me a briefing on what he had done to date and what was still required to be done. Colton, who was often away then to use up his accumulated leave before departing the service, suggested I spend a whole Sunday morning with him in the office for the briefing. I agreed. Colton was very nice and gave me a thorough briefing, passing me the relevant papers he had collected and those he had worked on towards the implementation plan. He took me to lunch at the Cellar Bar & Restaurant near Fullerton Building, and offered me a beer which I gratefully accepted. Following that briefing, and maybe the beer, I was able in due course to draw up a detailed implementation plan for the integration. In the event, the integration went rather well. Tan Chok Kian was pleased and commended me. He added that he believed the Minister, too, was happy. Following his retirement, Colton joined *The Straits Times* as personnel manager. In that capacity, some five years later, he invited me to take over from him so he could move on to another managerial position in the Straits Times Group.

Another interesting project Tan Chok Kian asked me to take charge of was the implementation of the policy decision for equal pay for women in the civil service. Up to then, there were separate pay scales for men and women. But rumours were rife that there was soon to be equal pay and service conditions for men and women in the civil service. Tan Chok Kian called me into his office one day and told me the equal pay policy was to be implemented very shortly, but that it was to remain secret till the appointed day itself. I collected the information required – much of it I had gathered already from my regular work and was quite familiar with – to draft in secret the implementation circular that would need to be issued for general information. Sitting down one night at home, with my required reference material at hand, I drafted by hand the implementation circular over the course of several hours. At the office the next morning, I had my draft circular faired and took it to my boss for clearance. He approved it and sent it on to the Minister for final approval, as required under the instruction manual. Following approval by the Minister, who raised no point nor query, the circular was issued in its final form in good time, with no leakage either, before the appointed date and time. My boss was delighted.

The union representing daily-rated employees including garbage and night soil collection workers of the former City Council, called a general strike of those workers. No collection and disposal of garbage or night soil could then be done by those workers during the strike. Since that could result in a serious health hazard, especially in a city like Singapore with a dense population, an emergency task force was quickly set up to take over that task. The task force was under the overall direction of expatriate officer Percival (Val) H Meadows of the Prime Minister's Office (PMO), who, like his compatriot Tony Colton, was due to depart the Singapore Civil Service under the Malayanisation programme. The workers of the task force, under armed Gurkha guard arranged by Val Meadows who had previously established good connection with the Gurkha command, carried out their task adequately during the strike. The Establishment Division of the Ministry of Finance was required to hold a watching brief throughout that strike and report on the operations of the task force and final outcome of the whole affair to our Minister. We were glad when it was all over. But the militant union led by K Suppiah went on to give more trouble later.

Val Meadows was initially in the Ministry of National Development when the PAP government first took office in 1959. Ong Eng Guan, who had been mayor in the City Council before it was disbanded and its responsibilities and functions integrated into the government, was then Minister for National Development. The story goes that, while on a visit with a team of officials from his ministry to a farm in a rural area of Singapore soon after taking up office as Minister for National Development, the Minister spoke to the farmer in the Minister's own Hokkien dialect, which was the most common dialect spoken in Singapore then. The farmer remained silent and shook his head. The Minister then tried Mandarin. Again, the farmer shook his head, muttering something which Val Meadows who was in that team recognised to be Cantonese. He immediately responded to the farmer in fluent Cantonese, then translated what the Minister had said to the farmer and the farmer's reply to the Minister. Val Meadows had, on first taking up appointment in the Singapore Civil Service under British rule, as was the custom and practice in the civil service then, been sent to Canton to live there for an extended period and learn Cantonese from native Cantonese speakers. Just as Tony Colton, about the same time, had similarly been sent to Amoy to learn Hokkien. The Minister did not say anything then, but turned abruptly on his heel and walked very quickly off, the whole team following as closely as they could behind. Possibly the Minister felt shamed by his own expat British officer, who could speak to and be understood by a local farmer, while he himself could not. Another factor could well have been the Minister's well-known antipathy to and mistrust of British expat officers while he was the Mayor of

Singapore. Not long after this incident, Val Meadows was posted to the Prime Minister's Office, where he remained till his due date for Malayanisation. Later, while on retirement in Singapore, he was called on to oversee a Gurkha contingent help quell a rebellion in Brunei shortly before formation of Malaysia, which Brunei in the event opted out of.

***

A Works Brigade had been set up soon after the PAP government took office. Camps of the brigade were set up to hold unemployed youths who would be deployed daily on various casual jobs, while awaiting employment in regular jobs in the government or elsewhere. Tan Chok Kian delegated me to represent the Finance Ministry on the management committee of the Works Brigade, with special regard to emplacement in regular jobs of those held in the camps. One day he sent me a file with a comment by the Minister against a regular report that had been sent to him that perhaps it was time to close the camps and disband the Works Brigade, as they did not seem to him to be fulfilling the role envisaged for them, and those held in the camps were apparently getting restless and possibly militant. Tan Chok Kian asked me what I thought. I responded that from my experience observing the Works Brigade and camps first hand, I felt the Works Brigade and camps could serve a useful purpose if certain changes, which I suggested, were made. Tan Chok Kian sent the file back to the Minister, with my suggestions and his support. The file very soon came back from the Minister with the terse command: "Do so, then!" The Works Brigade and camps lived on for some years after, though never really flourished. Minister Dr Goh Keng Swee was noted, especially in those early days, for his caustic, and sometimes very irreverent, comments. On one occasion, his Permanent Secretary (Perm Sec)

Oon Khye Kiang, whom the Minister did not particularly hold in any high regard nor got on any too well with, took a file he had got back from the Minister to his Deputy Secretary Lee Keng Tuan, who was a real man of the world and not one for mincing his words. The Perm Sec asked his deputy if he could help interpret a notation the Minister had made on a file. Below a submission the Perm Sec had made to the Minister, the Minister had drawn two circles side by side and initialled below. Lee Keng Tuan looked at the notation, then as he later reported to his colleagues, holding back his laughter, explained as politely as he could to the Perm Sec that the Minister's mark most likely meant "Balls!"

One day one of my officers handed me a letter he had received in the post offering a sum of money if the writer of the letter was given a job he had applied for. My officer asked what we should do with the letter, especially in view of the PM's own declared strong stand against corruption. The PM had declared publicly very early on that if he himself was corrupt, his Ministers would in turn be too, and it would go all the way down the line, till the postman would take the postage stamps off the letters. I took that letter with its patently corrupt offer of a bribe, though small, to my boss. He asked what I thought we should do. I replied that in view of the government's declared strong stand against corruption at all levels, the letter in question should be referred to the Corrupt Practices Investigation Bureau (CPIB) to take whatever action it deemed appropriate. My boss countered that since the job applied for was a low-paid one and the bribe offered was small, it was more than likely the letter writer would be young, poorly educated and not well off. Just referring the letter to the CPIB could well result in the letter writer being charged and convicted. In which case, he would carry that stigma the rest of his life, which probably still had a long way to go. I then suggested that in referring the case to the CPIB we should suggest the letter writer not be charged but called up by the CPIB to be advised where he had gone wrong and be warned not repeat such an act again. Which we did. The CPIB Director R B Corridon, spoke to my boss subsequently following receipt of the letter in question from us to thank us for our suggestion, which he thought very good and had carried out. As a result, he believed the young letter writer had been taught a good lesson he would not forget and would turn out better rather than worse in later life.

In the run-up to formation of Malaysia in 1963 and objection to Malaysia itself and Singapore joining it from an opposition political party in Singapore, the government decided to hold a referendum on Malaysia. In the event, the ballot paper for the referendum was such that it was really a choice as to the terms on which Singapore should join Malaysia rather than whether Singapore should join Malaysia at all. The opposition, on the other hand, contended the whole referendum was a sham. Since voting in Singapore is compulsory by law, the opposition found it difficult to advise the populace not to vote at all and threatened to canvass for blank or spoilt votes. The government threatened, in turn, to count blank or spoilt votes as votes in favour of Singapore joining Malaysia as a constituent state with the special terms for Singapore the latter had been able to extract from Malaya in the negotiations for the formation of Malaysia.

Several senior officers of the Singapore Civil Service, including me, were assigned to officiate at the voting centres and at the central counting centre when voting ended and all ballots were in. The central counting centre was at the Singapore Badminton Hall on Guillemard Road. Counting began at nightfall following the close of voting and collection and transportation of the sealed and well-secured ballot papers to the central counting centre, section by section in the counting hall, and went on and on for hours, with objections and recounts, till well into the next morning. The overall result of the count was in favour of Singapore joining Malaysia as a constituent state on the special terms the government had negotiated and agreed to in the negotiations, without taking in blank and spoilt votes. This was a result the government was most pleased with. It declared the following day a holiday for all who had worked so hard at the referendum and its voting centres and central counting centre. In the event, Singapore in Malaysia did not last too long, however.

***

My wife, Peggy Leong Wai Chee, was required to acquire recognised qualifications in library science for her job at the library of the then University of Malaya in Singapore. She applied for and was awarded a fellowship by the International House of the University of Chicago for an AM in librarianship at the University of Chicago, which I would jokingly refer to as a backward MA degree much to her displeasure and consternation. It was however regarded highly as a very good but tough course over two academic years, and she was required to be resident at the university for the entire two academic years. When she left for Chicago, she and I and our little daughter Karen, then just about eighteen months old, were living in our semi-detached house on Eden Grove, off Bartley Road, opposite the then New Country Hotel which mainly served British servicemen and their families on short assignment to Singapore or as interim living quarters for them before they moved on to more permanent living quarters. Karen and I then went to live with my parents in their home at 14 Parkstone Road. We remained there for some time with Peggy, on her return, before moving back to our home at Eden Grove following its renovation and rehabilitation, which it badly needed after it was rented out over the time Peggy was away, during which time it had been not at all been properly cared for.

One day, while still at the Ministry of Finance, the Minister's PA called me and told me the Minister wished to see me in his office, "Now!" I trotted over to the Minister's office and sat before him at his desk, as commanded. He smiled, which he was seldom seen to do without due provocation, then told me, "You are to work for the PM. Go over to his office at City Hall now. He'll tell you what you need to know about the job". The Minister would brook no questions. So, I took leave of the Minister and walked from the Fullerton Building across Cavanagh Bridge, through Empress Place, onto St Andrew's Road, then to City Hall and up to the second level, where the PM's office was. A Gurkha guard stood on duty on the landing outside the office and a security officer sat before a small table beside the Gurkha guard. I told the security officer who I was and why I was there. He scribbled something which I guessed had to be my name and where I was from and what I was there for onto his pad, then called someone from the phone on his desk, whom I presumed must be the PM's PA. I was then asked by the security officer to enter a small waiting room beside him that opened onto that landing on level two City Hall and wait there till summoned.

There were cushioned bench seats around three walls of the small waiting room, with a rectangular centre table and another smaller square table in a corner on which was a single telephone. There were no windows in the waiting room, only that single door through which I had entered and through which anyone in the room would have to exit.

VII
PMO & More

After a short while seated in that waiting room with nothing to occupy me except my thoughts, a man who looked to be in his mid-thirties, dressed in a white short-sleeved shirt and white trousers with black leather shoes, opened the door to the waiting room and summoned me by way of a hand gesture to follow him past the security officer seated at the small table and the Gurkha guard standing duty beside him through the main door and along the passageway leading to the PM's general office; past an office on the left with clear glass panels from waist high to the ceiling in which sat two men at their desks, clearly visible through the clear glass panels. One an elderly looking Chinese man and the other a not-so-old Malay man, whom I subsequently found were both political office holders in the PM's office, seated at two separate desks side by side with an aisle between them. Straight ahead, beyond that, was the PM's general office in which several officers were seated at separate desks, and a lone telephone operator sat at a small telephone exchange, against a floor to ceiling column, nearer the main entrance to the PM's office. The telephone operator could be clearly observed by the elderly Chinese and Malay men through the clear glass panels of their office and be clearly observed too at all times by those in the PM's general office. Thus, it was obvious, there could be a constant and most effective surveillance at all times by the elderly Chinese man and Malay man in their office as well as by those in the general office.

Leading me to a door on the right in the main passageway, the man I was following knocked once, firmly but not loudly, on a door and opened it, then said in a hushed but clearly audible voice, "Mr Hochstadt!" He then turned round without a word and left the way he had come, closing the door gently behind him and me. The PM, whom I easily recognised from his trademark white short-sleeved shirt and white trousers and from the several newspaper photos of him I had seen, beckoned me to sit on one of the two chairs across the highly polished and bare desk behind which he was seated. Not too long before I had also seen the PM at close quarters when he gave an evening talk at the University of Malaya campus at Bukit Timah to members of the university's Socialist Club following their detention on the grounds of subversion arising from an article in an edition of *Fajar*, the club's periodical, which, subsequently, was proscribed. On other occasions, too, on evening walks with a few fellow university students in the Botanical Gardens, a short walk from Bukit Timah campus along Cluny Road, we had come across the PM taking his children for evening walks through the Botanical Gardens.

The PM asked me, seated before him, if I knew why I was there in his office, and what I might be required to do, and expected of me. I said, "No", and added that the Finance Minister had told me I would be working for the PM and "to report immediately to the PM's office". So I had presumed that when I reported to the PM's office I would be told what would be required of me. The PM swivelled his chair round with a slight frown on his brow and silently stared through the large window into the distance, over the Padang and across to the Esplanade. After a few moments he swivelled his chair back to face me and asked, "Chinese, you know Chinese? You understand, speak, read and write Mandarin?" "No," I replied without hesitation. "Any Chinese dialects?" "No," again I responded. "Malay?" "I'm required to pass the government civil service Standard II exam in Malay for confirmation in my appointment and I passed Standard I some time ago but recently I was referred for Jawi in the Standard II exam," I replied. The PM looked at me intently, in silence, for a few seconds then said, "Should be no reason for you not to pass Jawi if you really put your mind to it and apply yourself diligently! Besides, it would be useful and advantageous to be able to read the editorials and commentaries in *Utusan Melayu*, which is in Jawi."

I did not say more and neither did the PM before he turned to the waist-high wooden cabinet lining the wall behind him on which were a number of telephones plus a single rather ancient looking intercom set. He pressed a button on the intercom then let it go without a word. Soon a man whom I recognised as the Cabinet Secretary entered the room through the door opening into the general office. "Yes, PM," he said. "Hochstadt here, as you know, is to be my Secretary, show him to the office Mr Barker occupied in the hallway before the Cabinet offices. He can occupy that office till all matters that need to be cleared are cleared and settled before taking up the appointment". "Yes, PM," said the Cabinet Secretary as he turned to walk out of the PM's office, beckoning me to follow him. He led me to a small office with just a desk and chair behind it and two visitors' chairs on the other side of the desk, with only a single telephone on that desk. This telephone, I was soon to discover only went through the telephone operator in the PM's office. There was clearly no entry to, nor exit from, that office except through the door that opened onto the second-level landing of City Hall between the PM's office and the Cabinet offices in full visibility of and observation by the security officer who might be on duty at the small desk there, as well as by the Gurkha guard standing duty there throughout; and no direct communication into or from that office except via that single telephone that only went through the telephone operator at the PM's office telephone exchange. And there was I marooned at the desk in that office for about a week, but seemingly much longer, till, as I later discovered after discreet enquiries, I had been accorded the required security clearance appropriate to the duties and responsibilities of a Secretary to PM.

Later, when I moved into my office within the PM's office, the Cabinet Secretary and I became good work colleagues and personal friends. Especially when I discovered his interest in film and introduced him to become a member of the Singapore Film Society of which I had a little earlier been elected president at the society's AGM. The Cabinet Secretary was also interested in motoring magazines and used to drop into my office from time to time for a chat and to borrow the motoring magazines I then subscribed to through the news vendor in a corner of a corridor on level one of City Hall whom I passed daily on the way between my office and the reserved carpark where I parked my Volvo 122S.

One of my first assignments as the PM's Secretary was to serve as secretary to the then newly set up Publicity and Propaganda Coordinating Committee (PPCC) of which the PM himself was chairman. Members of the committee included the Minister for Culture and his Political and Permanent Secretaries as well as the government Press Officer, K R S Vas, and the Director of Broadcasting, whose portfolio then took in the newly established TV service, as well as his Deputy. At one of the very first meetings of that committee in the PM's conference room, the PM asked me where certain pressmen were. I responded that I did not know which pressmen he sought and that they were supposed to be there and therefore they had not been invited to standby for any meeting with the PM. The PM immediately blew up and asked me very angrily and pointedly, "And why not?" I feebly replied that he had not asked me to tell them to standby, which caused the PM to get even hotter under his collar and bark, "I did. You forgot!" Which I well might have, especially with the abundance of new and unfamiliar work, much of which was required to have been done "yesterday" as officers in the PMO often declared, but could not admit to his having told me. He then added, "But even if I did not, do you think I have so much time to spare that I would just talk to my own Minister and Political Secretary and government officers about these issues and then say it again at some other meeting with the press later? Surely you've been in my office long enough to read my mind!" Before I could even attempt to answer the Press Officer, K R S Vas, came to the rescue and offered to call the missing pressmen himself, assuring the PM he could probably get them to the PM's conference room within fifteen minutes or so. He then dashed out to make his phone calls. He returned twenty minutes later with the two required pressmen in tow. In the interim, the PM continued his meeting with the rest of us, with a face contorted and red from his suppressed anger, while I had to remain as calm and collected as I could to diligently follow everything that was discussed so as to produce the draft minutes of that meeting within the standard twenty-four hours required by the PM for any draft minutes of his meetings.

That evening after work I went to the government Press Office on level one of City Hall to invite Vas over to the Singapore Cricket Club (SCC), across St Andrew's Road running along the length of the front of City Hall. Vas had already become a good friend of mine and we adjourned to the SCC from time to time for a few relaxing drinks of an evening after work with S T Ratnam, a former contemporary of mine from the university at Bukit Timah who then worked in the Ministry of Culture on level three of City Hall, as well as Francis D'Costa, another contemporary from the university who was then working in the main Prime Minister's Office on level one of City Hall.

It was about that time that the Sunday Constituency Tours for the PM began. These were usually whole day affairs starting off in the mornings around 1000 hours from the PM's home at 38 Oxley Road in a couple of Land Rovers with drivers fom the Primary Production Department under the Ministry of National Development: the first for the PM and his personal team including his security officers, and the second with me, my team, and a couple or so other officers from varying ministries and departments most relevant to the day's particular scheduled programme. My job was to be responsible, in conjunction with the relevant Legislative Assembly member and relevant community leaders, to plan, organise and implement each Sunday Constituency Tour and collect, register and collate petitions received by or on behalf of the PM, then refer each petition to the relevant government ministry, department or agency for whatever follow-up action might be needed and report back on the action taken, and ultimate reporting back on the action taken to each petitioner. There was no system then in the PM's office for this, so my able and most supportive colleague specially posted into the PM's office for this, young Higher Executive Officer (HEO), Frederick Ong, and later Lee Wai Kok who was posted in as my deputy, had to assist in developing and implementing a workable system. No easy task in those pre-computer days.

The first of those Sunday Constituency Tours was to the Jurong Constituency, which was then largely rural with farmers and squatters and not much else but chickens, ducks and pigs, farmed fish and Barisan Sosialis, the breakaway political party from the PAP in 1963, protesters. My team and I helped with the planning, organising and implementing of that tour but did not go on it ourselves. That was in the early days of internal self-government for Singapore when there was much debate amongst the older and more conservative senior officers of the public service as to what would be proper for public officers to do in direct support of their political leaders. There was a Deputy Secretary in the main PMO who originated from Malaya and joined the Singapore Civil Service and was sent in earlier days of British colonial rule on a training programme in the UK on diplomacy in the days when Singapore was in a political limbo before becoming a state of Malaysia, who was of a strictly conservative frame of mind in regard to such matters. He made clear to me that he would not go on the tour himself as it would not be proper for a civil servant to do so because it was a political activity, and most strongly advised that I should not do so either for sake of propriety. So I took heed and did not go myself and told my team in the PM's office that they need not go either. Next day the Legislative Assembly member for Jurong whom by then I had got to know quite well personally, popped over to the PM's office first thing in the morning to warn me the PM had been asking for me on that Sunday Constituency Tour to Jurong and I had better prepare myself to answer to the PM when he turned up in office. But the PM's PA told me, following his visit to PM's home with the box of office papers for the PM to work on at home as the PM had been tired out by the Sunday Constituency Tour, that the PM had asked him while he was at the PM's house with the latter's papers, why I had not gone on the tour to Jurong the previous day as I should have as part of my duties and responsibilities as his Secretary. Later I was advised by the PM himself that I was expected to accompany him without fail for the remaining Sunday Constituency Tours and had better make sure I did for all the remaining ones. Which of course I did without fail.

Following that very first Sunday Constituency Tour to Jurong, I made very sure I did not only take responsibility for the overall planning, organising and implementing whatever might need to be implemented for each and every such tour that followed, I joined each Sunday tour as well, right to the very last. The last two tours had to be held together, back-to-back, on the same Sunday immediately following the PM's return from London, where discussions on the impending formation of Malaysia were being held. This was necessary to comply with the law in regard to no campaigning from midnight on the eve of polling day to polling day itself. The last two-in-one Sunday Constituency Tour was therefore quite a strain on the PM and on all of us other Sunday Constituency Tour regulars. It was a great relief though, when we finished the last of those back-breaking Sunday tours.

The tours in the series to the Southern Islands and to Pulau Tekong I found very interesting and most memorable. To get to the Southern Islands, we had to muster at the Master Attendant's pier along Collyer Quay, beside Clifford Pier, and embark on the three launches laid on by the Master Attendant. We were escorted by two Marine Police vessels. It was interesting going by Pulau Brani to see what was reported to be the last Orang Laut or Sea Gypsy village in Singapore on stilts over the water. Arriving at the first island of that tour to the Southern Island chain, the tide was out and there was no pier there, so we had to roll up our trousers and wade through the knee-high water to shore. The press photographers on that tour of course had a field day, taking candid shot after candid shot of the PM, accompanied by his Secretary and security officers wading through the water with their trouser legs rolled up. They splashed those photos on the front pages of their newspapers the next day.

This, of course led to many far-from-favourable comments about the skinny legs of the PM and of his Secretary as well. But it also drew a petition from the islanders for a pier at their island that they had asked for before but never got. That petition was most speedily dealt with and satisfied in record time.

On the tour to Pulau Tekong sometime later, the Marine Police officer-in-charge (OC), on the lead of the two Marine Police escort vessels, was Charles Bridges, a good friend of mine who had been introduced to me by my brother-in-law, Derrick de Souza, a police officer and OC Security at the time. By the end of that tour to Pulau Tekong, which entailed much walking on shore to the various kampongs, it was already evening and turning to dusk. Charlie decided it would be best, for reasons of security and the easier traffic along the roads, for us to disembark at Changi and drive thence to the PM's home and on from there to our respective destinations. However, while the PM, his security officers and immediate entourage, including my team and I, would disembark from this alternative pier decided on by Charlie, the rest of the main entourage would disembark according to the original plan at the Master Attendant's pier, from which they had embarked that morning. I informed the PM of the proposed change and got his OK, then notified Charlie to go ahead with arrangements for the change. Which he did by getting the wireless operator on his Marine Police escort vessel to radio the Police Radio Division Operations Room ashore at Police HQ on Pearl's Hill to pass on the notification to all concerned and also notify the telephone operator at the Istana telephone exchange, on duty 24/7, to arrange for the PM's official car and driver to go to the pier at which the PM's party would disembark. But, when the PM's launch docked at that pier, his assigned car and driver were nowhere to be seen. Charlie quickly ascertained that the driver, not having been to that pier before nor having the opportunity to check the route in advance, had got lost but was now well on his way to the freshly designated pier and would be another fifteen minutes or so. I informed the PM and he quite calmly and cheerily, and not as I expected, asked me to get him a bottle of beer to quench his thirst while we waited. I did not know where to get a bottle of beer from around there, so sought Charlie's help. Charlie immediately responded, "No problem, leave it to me," and dashed off in one of the police cars standing by. He soon returned with a cold bottle of beer, a glass and a bottle opener on a tray. I took the tray with the bottle of beer, the glass and bottle opener to the PM who opened the bottle and poured himself a glass. I told the PM, "OC Marine Police, Charles Bridges, got the beer for you and paid for it." The PM told me to thank Charlie for him and enjoined me to reimburse Charlie through the office as usual the next day. To which I said, "Yes, PM," but later, when I told Charlie about the reimbursement, he shook his head and, with a big grin and wink, said, "Never mind, you can buy me a beer some time."

The following week I promptly invited Charlie to join me for a beer, his favourite drink, at the Victoria Bar & Restaurant, one of Charlie's favourite haunts and part of the Victoria Hotel on Victoria Street and invited a couple of my good friends to join us. Charlie was thrilled. While we were there, he showed off his trick: while sitting at the table with an unopened bottle of beer on the table before him, he would bend over while still seated on his chair with his hands clasped behind his back, and take the bottle between his teeth, bite off the bottle cap and spit it out, then take the open bottle between his teeth, lift up his head and gulp down the entire contents of the bottle in one go, then place the empty bottle back onto the table and lean back in his chair with the biggest possible smile on his face. He performed to the acknowledgement and acclaim of all those around. During that session at Victoria Bar & Restaurant, Charlie, who was in his element, spoke in his native Hainanese dialect to the bar proprietor and waitresses, who were Hainanese. Charlie's mother was Hainanese and his father was from Britain, arriving in Singapore with the British forces after World War II, then taking up employment as Superintendent of the Victoria Theatre in Empress Place. And a most capable and popular Superintendent of Victoria Theatre he was, as most readily attested to by my father, who was a keen member of the Singapore Teachers' Union Drama Group and took lead roles in amateur Shakespearean theatricals put on by that group at the Victoria Theatre. After rehearsals and performances at the Victoria Theatre, they would all go with Charlie's father for supper and drinks at Bugis Street.

During the course of those Sunday Constituency Tours, I had on some occasions to fly to Kuala Lumpur (KL) to meet the PM, Mrs Lee and others, including on many occasions the Cabinet Secretary, while they were in transit at KL on their return flight to Singapore by BOAC. On one of those occasions, Mrs Lee and the PM queried me at great length on the recent riot on the penal settlement of Pulau Senang during which the superintendent of that penal settlement, an expatriate prison officer named Duxton, had been killed by the inmates, and had his eyes gouged out and his genitals chopped off and stuffed into his mouth. Mrs Lee, in particular, expressed much grief and horror over that whole most unfortunate affair. The penal settlement on Pulau Senang had been set up following the report of a Commission of Inquiry under the chairmanship of C V Devan Nair who later became President of the Republic of Singapore. Devan Nair himself had been a political detainee on St John's Island and was released in 1959 by the PAP. He had been a teacher at St Andrew's School immediately before his detention and my younger brother, Carl, was a student then in his class. Devan Nair was also a member of the Singapore Teachers' Union and its Drama Group with my father.

In the early days of the setting up of the penal settlement on Pulau Senang, my immediate boss in the Establishment Division of the Ministry of Finance, Tan Chok Kian, was invited to make an inspection tour on behalf of the Budget Division of the Ministry of Finance of the new penal settlement and had asked me to go along. I recall, while walking along a path in single file behind my boss and Superintendent Duxton, that as we walked past an inmate squatting on the manicured lawn on the side of the path, clipping the already short grass with a pair of large but ordinary house scissors, which I thought most unusual and inappropriate for the job, he turned his head sideways to look up at Duxton with glazed eyes full of more animal hate than I had ever encountered. Only once before, during the Japanese Occupation, had I seen a similar look but with far less hatred. When, a few days following the death of my maternal grandfather, John Phillips, in the POW ward of the general hospital, my Uncle Stanley turned up at 14 Parkstone Road, in the back of a small truck driven by a Malay civilian driver and a Japanese soldier in the back to guard the few POWs there, including my Uncle Stanley. They had been out from the POW camp on some mission, following which on the way back to camp, as they were going along Tanjong Katong Road, Uncle Stanley managed to sweet-talk the guard into diverting the truck to 14 Parkstone Road so Uncle Stanley could make a brief visit to see his mother, Grandma Helen Phillips, to console her on the passing away of her husband. After Uncle Stanley had gone up to Grandma's room, where she lay in bed paralysed from a stroke, to briefly console her, he sat for while in the dining room with my mother and father to chat. My father served Uncle Stanley a mug of steaming black coffee made from doubtful coffee grounds, the only kind available then and only from the black market. Uncle Stanley then asked my father to make another cup of coffee for me to offer to the Japanese guard in the truck out of courtesy and in gratitude for allowing Uncle Stanley to visit his mother, which I did. A female POW there gave me such a hateful, animal stare for, she must have felt, treating the Japanese guard at all like another human being.

***

What struck me most on those Sunday Constituency Tours was how, once the PM warmed up and really got going, onstage before an audience, he could gauge their mood and swing it from not-too-friendly to a friendly and cheering crowd. The PM was fluent then in both English and Malay but not Mandarin nor Hokkien, the latter being the main Chinese dialect in Singapore. On those tours to the constituencies he would usually have his Mandarin tutor along, and Hokkien tutor too on occasion when he thought the population mix of the particular constituency required it. These tutors would travel in the same Land Rover as the PM and help guide him along, quietly and unobtrusively at stops along the way. The PM had learnt well the efficacy of television in politics and, especially, election campaigns from the presidential election campaign of John F Kennedy whom many had initially derided as a lost cause in view of his being a Roman Catholic and an overtly practicing one too. In fact, keeping or turning the mood of the electorate from going sour in the run-up to the general election before Malaysia itself was a prime reason driving the hurried start-up of the very first television station and service in Singapore.

At the very first of those Sunday Constituency Tours, the PM had promised he would visit every constituency on that series of tours prior to the next general election. Tours to the last two constituencies still remained when nomination and then polling day for the general election were declared. Election campaigning had, by law, to end by midnight of the eve of polling day. But the PM had to make another of his representative sessions in London pre-Malaysia, leaving just one Sunday to tour two constituencies. The PM decided he and his team would return from that session of the Malaysia talks in London on the Saturday for a good night's sleep and rest at home before going on that gruelling last two-in-one Sunday Constituency Tour. I was ordered to fly to KL carrying some office papers and the previous week's Singapore daily newspapers for the PM, and to brief him during his transit stop on the plans and programme for that very last two-in-one Sunday Constituency Tour and on whatever else the PM might require me to. I flew to KL on the Friday and checked into the Embassy Hotel, then called my good friend from university, Sarjit Singh. He had quit the Singapore Civil Service a few years earlier to take up appointment as administrative officer in the Rubber Research Institute in KL to be with his wife Jasbir who had herself taken up an academic career in the Faculty of Education at the University of Malaya in Kuala Lumpur. We arranged to meet that evening at the Colonial Bar & Restaurant for drinks and dinner with Sarjit's brother-in-law, Dr Satwant Singh, elder brother of Jasbir. Satwant had been an outstanding student of zoology in the Zoology Department of the University of Malaya at Bukit Timah during the time both Sarjit and I were there and had won scholarships to further his studies. We had a jolly time that night with friends of Sarjit or Satwant joining us from time to time. In the very early hours of the next morning, Satwant drove me back to my hotel and then Sarjit to his home in Petaling Jaya before returning to his own home. We agreed to meet again the next day after I had seen the PM and his entourage off at Subang Airport in KL for Singapore following their BOAC transit there.

I met the PM and entourage at KL airport the next day to hand over the office papers and newspapers and to brief the PM on the next day's two-in-one Sunday Constituency Tour, then retreated to join the others in the adjoining room, leaving the PM to read his office papers and newspapers. The Cabinet Secretary, who was in the room with the others, tried to persuade me to return to Singapore from KL on the same BOAC flight as the PM and party so I could be at hand to answer the PM should the PM require anything from me on the flight. But I told the Cabinet Secretary I could not as I had already made arrangements to meet up for dinner with some former colleagues and friends in KL and had booked to return to Singapore on the last flight back that night. After the PM and entourage had boarded their return flight to Singapore, I got the official car and driver based at Singapore House in KL, which had taken me and my baggage to the airport earlier, to drop me and my baggage at the Colonial Bar & Restaurant at which Sarjit and Satwant had agreed we would meet that evening. Late that night Satwant, accompanied by Sarjit, dropped me and my baggage off at KL airport, which I found to my consternation to be rather dark and deserted. When I got to where the check-in should have been, I found it closed and the last flight to Singapore already departed. So I found some place to sit quietly and have a snooze while waiting for the check-in counter to open and check-in for the first flight to Singapore. The bar, restaurant and even coffee shop at the airport were all closed for the night. I checked-in for the first flight to Singapore that morning and got into Singapore and home at 14 Parkstone Road, only to be told by my brother-in-law Derrick, who lived with his wife, my younger sister Joan, and children with my parents at 14 Parkstone Road, that there had been a call for me from the Istana telephone operator who, when told by Derrick that I had not yet returned from KL but was expected back soon, asked that I be informed that the PM had called for a meeting at his home that morning in regard to the day's tour programme. My attendance was expected at that meeting before we all left on the tour itself. I hurriedly had a shower and changed before driving to the PM's house. I really do not know how I managed to get through that last Sunday Constituency Tour, catching brief snoozes along the way, in the second Land Rover of the convoy, between designated stops. We finished just before midnight, to a great cheer from the whole team at having delivered on the promise made at the very start!

Besides the Sunday Constituency Tours leading up to the general election, there was much else going on to fully engage and occupy the mind and muscle of the PM and his office in the midst of that critical period in the history of Singapore compressed into the few years between 1959 and 1965 – of which I served as the PM's Secretary from 1962 to 1965. First, there was the election of the PAP to the fully elected Legislative Assembly and assumption of power by the PAP in 1959 as the government of the internal self-governing State of Singapore and dissolution of the former City Council. Then there was the split in the ruling party in the government of the State of Singapore and formation of the splinter Barisan Sosialis, which became a most strident opposition to the government in the Legislative Assembly and the last general election to the Legislative Assembly in 1963 before Singapore became a constituent state of Malaysia. Malaysia was formally established in mid-September 1963, set originally for 31 August 1963, Malayan Merdeka Day, but postponed while a United Nations Commission set about interviewing representatives and residents of Sabah and Sarawak to ascertain whether they really favoured the concept of Malaysia and Sabah and Sarawak being taken in as component states – the State of Singapore excluded, since it had already voted in its own Malaysian Referendum in favour of

Malaysia with Singapore as a constituent state. The PM, seeking to ensure there was no reversion on the part of Singapore should Malaysia as conceived be aborted or stillborn, went ahead on 31 August 1963 with his unilateral declaration of independence for Singapore. And during Sukarno's Konfrontasi acts of aggression including the planting of bombs by two Indonesian commandos in MacDonald House on Orchard Road near the Istana, which killed a secretary of a branch of the Hong Kong & Shanghai Bank that occupied the ground floor and other floors of MacDonald House; the landing of Indonesian troops on Singapore's mangrove-covered west coast who were found there, dispirited, early one morning by a small police search force from the Tanjong Pagar Police Station, under which police divisional jurisdiction that area lay, led by Police Deputy Superintendent A Gopalan who was a good friend of mine; the surprise attack one early morning in the jungle of Kota Tinggi, in the Malaysian State of Johore, on a platoon from the 1st Battalion of the Singapore Regiment who were cooling off in a stream while on patrol, and killing a few while injuring some others; the consequent formation of a civilian volunteer Vigilante Corps mooted by DPM Dr Toh Chin Chye to serve as the ears and eyes of the civil population of Singapore against infiltration into Singapore of Indonesian "terrorists" – since Sukarno had not declared war against Malaysia nor even Singapore – because defence, internal security and foreign affairs and hence the army, navy, air force and police were the direct responsibility of the central government of Malaysia in KL. There was also the campaign led by Singapore's DPM and Minister for Culture, both originally from Malaya, for a "Malaysian Malaysia". The country also experienced the racial riots of 1963 and 1964, which added significant push towards the Separation of Singapore from Malaysia on 9 August 1965. All of these events, no doubt, put the PM under severe strain far in excess of the consequent stress that Lee Wai Kok, I and others in the PM's office had to endure.

After a few continuous days being subjected to such daily strain, one evening while at home after work at my parents' house at 14 Parkstone Road, I took out my old Underwood portable typewriter, on which I had taught myself to touch-type while a temporary clerk at the Teachers' College at Cairnhill Road before I started university, and typed out a letter of resignation on a sheet of plain white paper. I put the letter into a plain white envelope, with no name nor address on the envelope, since I intended to hand the letter to the PM's PA the next morning for him in turn to pass on to the PM. I knew from experience on the job that it was standard operating procedure that all items of correspondence for the PM be taken out of their envelopes, which were put aside, before the contents themselves were passed on to the PM. After I handed the letter of resignation to the PM's PA the next morning, he told me he had just received a call from the PM who said he would not come into office that day as he was tired out by the multiple official events and special occasions he had to officiate at and attend the previous day, and that evening he had to officiate at the foundation stone laying ceremony for Jurong Primary School. The PM told the PA to bring him whatever office papers that needed to be dealt with. The PA assured me he would put my letter with the office papers that were to be taken to the PM's home. Later the PA reported the PM had asked him, "What is this all about?" when the PA handed him my letter of resignation. I assured the PA that I would myself explain to the PM at the office the next day.

That evening at the foundation stone laying ceremony for Jurong Primary School, which I had planned to attend as the petition for that school was amongst the very first petitions received on the very first Sunday Constituency Tour. I stood with the crowd at the site of the foundation stone laying ceremony for Jurong Primary School. The PM, after alighting from the official car accompanied by his personal security officer, walked to where he was to officiate at the ceremony, and asked as he approached me, "So, what's it all about?" I immediately responded, "Not here, PM, in office!" The PM said no more but continued on his way to the designated officiating spot, smiling and waving to supporters in the crowd as he went by.

An incident I recall which shows how well the PM could control himself to effect results he wanted was when a delegation from the Australian Labor Party led by Gough Whitlam and invited to Singapore by the PM arrived for a reception at Sri Temasek, the PM's official residence in the grounds of the Istana. As the delegation was about to enter Sri Temasek, I rushed up to open the door for them, but pulled the door in instead of pushing it out, which caused the door to snag against the carpeted floor. The PM then calmly opened the door himself, pushing it out and before greeting his guests gave me a sweet smile while muttering to me under his breath what a fool I was for pulling the door in rather than pushing it out. Later Whitlam quietly said to me in private, "I see the PM seems to like you a lot. I noticed he gave you a very nice smile when you tried to open the door for us just now." I just smiled and nodded my head in response, not wanting to admit to Whitlam that the PM knew only too well that if he wanted his Secretary to be effective, he had to show others that he had confidence in his own Secretary

The day after the stone laying ceremony, the PM buzzed me into his office first thing on the intercom. I went to his office to find him standing beside his desk with his short-sleeved white shirt off and white singlet too, wiping his sweaty body with a small white towel. He then put the towel aside and tucked a fresh white singlet into his trousers. He asked once more, "What's this all about?" pointing to my letter, the only thing very conspicuously on the PM's shiny and otherwise bare desk. "The strain, PM … too much!" I replied. "What strain?" he immediately demanded, "If anyone around here has strain, it is me! But we have to carry on, not just give up like that. It's for our very survival … and that of Singapore!" I realised deep down that what the PM said was very true, but I remained silent. "You're tired!" the PM added, tucking in his white shirt. "Take the day off. Go, get a good rest … and take this with you." He slid my letter across his shiny bare desk. I took the letter, walked back to my desk, cleared pending immediate and urgent office work, then walked to my Volvo 122S in the City Hall car park and drove to the Ban Chuan Bar & Restaurant on Orchard Road beside the Royal Thai Consulate, which stood on large grounds purchased on Siamese King Chulalongkorn's very first overseas trip. I then made a few calls on a house telephone of Ban Chuan Bar & Restaurant to try to summon some good friends to join me there for lunch and a few beers to give good cheer. But, just as I had got started, the manager of the restaurant summoned me to another house phone to answer a call from the Istana telephone operator. In those pre-mobile phone days, the PM's Secretary as well as other similarly designated officers too were required to leave a phone number where they could be contacted at any time wherever they might be by the PM himself or by anyone on his behalf. The Istana telephone operator told me he had a call from the PM's PA to ask me to return to the office immediately by order of the PM himself. "But the PM told me to take the day off!" I protested to the Istana telephone operator. "Sorry, I don't know about that," said the Istana telephone operator apologetically. "But, I think you had better report to the office straight away." I rushed back to City Hall. When I got there I went directly to the PM's room and said, "Yes, PM?" "There's urgent work to be done," the PM immediately responded. "Here, take these papers, read them … I'll call you in later to tell you what to do," he said as he handed me a bunch of papers marked "SECRET". I took the large brown envelope with its bunch of papers, walked back to my desk and began to read.

The racial riots of 1963 were a particularly trying time for us in the PM's office. My fellow Secretary to the PM, Lee Wai Kok, ably assisted by our HEO, Frederick Ong, had to be the principal liaison between the PM's office, representing the government, and the legislative assemblymen and other designated consituency representatives. This included the passing on of directives and messages and issuing curfew passes to the assemblymen and designated others so they could go about their business of representing the constituents and their interests even during curfew hours if necessary. Often there would be queues in the office of those seeking curfew passes for themselves or on behalf of others. Both Wai Kok and Fred had to remain calm and collected in the face of impatient assemblymen and their representatives. Wai Kok, ably assisted by Fred, had to first confirm the identity of the supplicants and establish their eligibility for curfew passes, then register the name of each person to whom a pass was to be issued, as well as the registration number of the pass and date and time of issue. While I, in addition to the usual duties and responsibilities of the first Secretary to the PM, had to also take my turn as civilian liaison officer in the operational headquarters of the Police Radio Division HQ at Pearls' Hill, with in turn Francis D'Costa from the administrative division of the main PMO and S T Ratnam of the Ministry of Culture. In my role as Secretary to the PM, I had on occasion to also go to the Paya Lebar Airport VIP room to assist the Malaysian Ministry for External Affairs representative office in Singapore in welcoming Malaysian VIPs visiting or in transit through Singapore. On one occasion, I had to assist in receiving the Malaysian Deputy Prime Minister (DPM), Tun Abdul Razak, on a visit to Singapore to tour, with his entourage, riot-affected areas and the big Malay enclave of Geylang Serai, but he said not a word to me nor even acknowledged my presence as an official representative of Singapore, a constituent state of Malaysia, and just walked by with cane in hand, whispering gravely to members of his entourage.

But there were lighter moments for me too then. On one occasion after an afternoon session of duty at the police wireless operations room I drove in my Volvo 122S to Paya Lebar Airport to meet my good friends, Francis D'Costa and S T Ratnam, who were not on duty at the police operational headquarters that evening. We had agreed to meet in the bar and lounge of Paya Lebar Airport, which was one of the few open during curfew hours. When I got there I found both Francis and S T sitting, with drinks on their table, talking animatedly to the great jazz trumpeter, Louis Armstrong, who happened to be in transit at Singapore for several hours and could not go to a hotel nor anywhere else in town owing to the curfew, so had taken to the bar and lounge at Paya Lebar Airport to while away those several hours. Francis suddenly pulled a notebook out from his pocket and asked Louis Armstrong to pen an autograph for him on a blank page of the notebook. Louis Armstrong smilingly complied. S T then did similarly, which Louis Armstrong also smilingly agreed to. Realising I did not have any such notebook myself, I pulled a $1 note from my trouser pocket and proffered it to Louis Armstrong to autograph. Louis Armstrong took the $1 note from me and asked with a devilish smile, "Only $1?" I said, "Yes, that's all I can afford … I'm a Singapore civil servant!" Louis Armstrong did not say more but smilingly autographed my $1 note and handed it back to me saying, "Keep it well, some day it may be worth $1 million!" I did keep that $1 note autographed by the great Louis Armstrong well, but after several moves of house and home over the years it was lost, never again to be seen by me.

We got over those riots and not too long after came the separation of Singapore from Malaysia on 9 August 1965. Just before that day, the PM and his family flew to KL to stay for a few days at Singapore House before moving on to the Cameron Highlands for a short break. Meanwhile, there were goings and comings between Singapore and KL by the Finance Minister and the Minister for Law. On one such occasion, following his return from KL, the Finance Minister called me on the phone and chided me for having revealed to the press he had gone to KL and when he would return. As, complained the Finance Minister, on his return a few reporters were in the airport VIP room waiting for him. I denied having tipped off the press, as was indeed the case, but the Finance Minister obviously disbelieved me. From then on there was no request from him or his office to book flights out or in, nor to arrange the VIP room for him, the usual responsibilities of the PM's office. I later discovered he had made his own arrangements for the booking of his flights and a car and driver to send him and his security officer right up to the boarding stairs on the tarmac and pick him up from there on his return.

On the morning of 9 August 1965, I got a call from the Istana telephone operator that the PM wanted me early that morning. I did as was bid wondering all the while when the PM and family had got back from the Cameron Highlands as I had not been informed of their return as I usually would have been. Immediately when the PM got to the office he buzzed for me. He told me to arrange for the representatives of the Commonwealth countries based in Singapore to get to City Hall by a set time and for me to take them immediately to the waiting room on level two that I had myself been held in on my initial call at the PM's office, which could only be accessed through the single door opening onto the landing between the PM's office and the Cabinet offices. That room was served by a single telephone, which could receive or send only through the telephone operator in the PM's office. There the Commonwealth representatives were to wait till summoned. He then asked me to follow him to the waiting room itself, picked up the telephone handset, unscrewed the speaker cap, took out the diaphragm within, then screwed the cap back on and replaced the handset on the base of its cradle. That telephone could thus receive but not call out. He then instructed me to ensure the radio and TV transmitting station on Bukit Batok would be operational and able to transmit at all times. Then left me to do as I was bid. From my office I first called the officer in charge of the Bukit Batok transmitting station, whom I fortunately happened to have been introduced to some time before by my cousin, Jack Phillips, who had been a fellow student of his at the Technical College in KL, and passed on the message to ensure that transmitting station was operational at all times. I then called or left messages for the various Commonwealth representatives based in Singapore, except for the British Deputy High Commissioner as I had been instructed, to present themselves at the PM's office by the designated time. While doing that I got a call through the PM's office telephone operator that the British High Commissioner himself, based in KL, wished to speak to me. When I took the call, the British High Commissioner told me he had to speak to the PM urgently but could not seem to be able to do so though he believed the PM was in Singapore. I told the British High Commissioner that as far as I was aware the PM and his family were in the Cameron Highlands or on their way back as the official car and driver had not yet as far as I knew returned to Singapore. The British High Commissioner retorted angrily, "Not likely! He is in Singapore! I need to speak with him personally most urgently!" I responded,

"Sorry, I can't help you!" The British High Commissioner hung up on me without another word. Later, when I briefed the PM on this, he did not say anything but just smiled to himself. However, when the PM briefed the press later on the Separation, he repeated my story, adding that his Secretary had to resort to pulling a fast one on the British High Commissioner who was trying to get through to the PM to put a stop to Separation. To my utter chagrin! The upshot for me of that whole episode was that I missed the meeting of the PM with the Commonwealth representatives based in Singapore. I also missed the PM's press briefing that followed immediately after in the old City Hall chamber, during which the PM broke down and wept, causing him to adjourn that press briefing to later that day. Meanwhile, I sat alone and forlorn in my little room at the PM's office holding fort there with not much to do. I missed that momentous occasion, while being within spitting range of it. As I did again later when I missed the historic formal admission of the Republic of Singapore to the United Nations as an independent and full member.

VIII

United Nations in New York, London, Nairobi, Dar-es-Salaam, Lusaka, Kampala, Blantyre, Cairo, Tunis, Algiers, Paris, Belgrade, Moscow, New Delhi, Rangoon, Phnom Penh & Bangkok

Immediately on Separation, the new Ministry of Foreign Affairs (MFA) and Ministry of Interior & Defence (MID) were set up. The former Minister for Culture became the Minister for Foreign Affairs and had his ministry's headquarters (HQ) at City Hall, while MID initially had its HQ at the government offices at

Empress Place while the Minister, who insisted on being referred to as the Minister of Defence, temporarily ensconced himself and his personal staff in offices at the Finance Ministry at the Fullerton Building. Later, once office space at the Police HQ on Pearl's Hill was made available and redesigned and renovated to suit the Minister's and MID's requirements, the Minister's office and entire MID HQ too moved into Pearl's Hill, where the Commissioner of Police and his staff also held fort.

MFA was tasked amongst its very first prime responsibilities to get the new Republic of Singapore admitted as a newborn sovereign and independent nation membership of the United Nations (UN). And, in pursuit of the objective of getting recognition of the new republic and its acceptance as an independent and sovereign friend by as many nations as it could in the shortest time possible, it was deemed expeditious that a goodwill mission should go following admission of the Republic of Singapore's membership of the UN to several countries in Africa, essentially those in the Commonwealth and the Non-Aligned Movement; and on to Eastern Europe, South Asia and Southeast Asia. The plan was for the mission to go to the UN in New York, and thence on to Kenya, Tanzania, Zambia, Uganda, Malawi, Egypt, Tunisia, Algeria, Yugoslavia, the USSR, India, Burma, Cambodia and Thailand with a side visit after Cambodia to Ceylon for the Foreign Minister and his PA. An estimated itinerary by air for the main delegation with just a couple of days in each capital city that added up to some two months plus of continuous travel, living in hotels and such accommodation when not housed as state guests in official accommodation, and out of not more than one suitcase each for the entire itinerary. As it was by then already past mid August, we had to act fast to be in time for the UN Security Council meeting and UN General Assembly in New York in September that year, 1965. It fell to me, as Secretary to the PM in the days of the State of Singapore, to deal with Commonwealth and other country representation on behalf of the PM and the State of Singapore, to plan and arrange for this as well as to make air travel and accommodation bookings for the PM, ministers, and other members of the delegation. I was also specially assigned from the PM's office to accompany the delegation for the entire journey as its Administrative Secretary as a precursor, I was told, to my then being officially posted fom the PM's office to MFA.

The mission was led by DPM Dr Toh Chin Chye who continued in those days of the Republic as DPM and Foreign Minister S Rajaratnam. The PM wrote personally to the leaders of a number of those countries to be visited, particularly the members of the Non-Aligned Movement, with whom he had established cordial relations earlier, to briefly set out the objectives and purpose of the mission and seek their support and assistance for the mission. The Foreign Minister wrote similarly to the Malaysian Permanent Representative to the UN in New York, R Ramani, for support and assistance at the UN Security Council meeting and General Assembly, which the Prime Minister of Malaysia, Tunku Abdul Rahman, had already pledged as a corollary of the Separation agreement. Ambassador R Ramani and his team did in the event extend exemplary support and assistance to our mission. Such support did prove most helpful in that there was no objection at all in the Security Council and General Assembly to the Republic of Singapore's UN membership. In my capacity as Administrative Secretary, I wrote to, among others, Singapore's Trade Representative in London, G F A Hibbert, who had been an expatriate officer in the Trade Department of the Singapore Civil Service pre-1959. From Hibbert I sought his support and assistance in following up with the various diplomatic and consular representatives in London of the countries in the mission's planned itinerary. Hibbert turned out to be most valuable at a time when Singapore was completely lacking in diplomatic and consular representation. His personal approach in London for the various sought and hoped for appointments and meetings did undoubtedly contribute most significantly to success for that mission.

On my part, getting things going from the Singapore end also involved contacting an old friend and former fellow student at the University of Malaya at Bukit Timah, who was then in senior management at the BOAC main office in Singapore to assign one of his senior officers who happened by choice rather than accident to have also been a student at and graduate of the University of Malaya at Bukit Timah to work with me on planning the detailed itinerary for the entire mission including the required travel and helping arrange for accommodation in the various countries we were to visit other than for those countries where accommodation was to be provided to the team as state guests. I also got in touch with my good friend, Thomas Abraham, Deputy Indian High Commissioner in Singapore, who had been earlier introduced to me by Press Officer K R S Vas who was a friend of his and who sometimes joined Vas and me for after office hours drinks of an evening, to notify the Indian diplomatic offices in the capital cities of the countries of our visits to extend whatever support and assistance they could to the mission on its travels, particularly in Africa, Moscow and, of course, of the central government itself in New Delhi. Which also proved to be most helpful and useful. K R S Vas, kindly also introduced, me over drinks one evening, to the newly appointed USSR TASS correspondent in Singapore, Sergei Severin, who had earlier been based in Bangkok and who most kindly offered his support and assistance for the entire mission in Moscow. He even went ahead to Moscow himself and personally accompanied the delegation while in Moscow to the October Revolution celebrations in the Red Square and to the Bolshoi Ballet and to some official receptions as well. Vas and Severin proved most useful and were good company of an evening to boot.

From Singapore we headed for the US west coast and on from there to New York, a total journey wih no stopovers of some thirty-six hours in all. But our flight to Hong Kong was diverted to Taipei owing to an accident on the runway at Kai Tak Airport resulting in closure of the runway. The Republic of China was one of the first to officially convey recognition of the new Republic of Singapore, which Singapore had not acknowledged. But the Captain of our Malayan Airways flight had been instructed by MFA HQ through the Malayan Airways HQ in Singapore to seek approval from Taipei for us to transfer at Taipei, through which Malayan Airways did not have traffic rights. High-level official representatives of the Taipei government were at the airport to receive our delegation, the newly appointed Permanent Secretary to the Singapore Foreign Ministry, Abu Bakar bin Pawanchee who was himself a member of the Singapore delegation, had got the captain of our flight to also radio on ahead to Taipei to notify them the DPM and Foreign Minister of the new Republic of Singapore would be on board and of our delegation's unexpected call at Taipei, owing to the problem at Hong Kong airport, and seeking assistance from the Taipei authorities for the delegation's unexpected transit at Taipei while an alternative flight to Tokyo was arranged. The Taipei officials were most accommodating and helpful, providing official cars and a small bus and van to carry the whole delegation and baggage to a nearby state-owned hotel to transit, refresh themselves and drink and eat there as well as keep our delegation company at the hotel and ensure we were well taken care of while a suitable alternative flight for the was arranged. Then transport the whole delegation and baggage back to the airport in Taipei for the flight to Tokyo and see our delegation and baggage safely off to Tokyo. Other than that, the flights were uneventful – the gods must have thought we had more than enough excitement – and we arrived at our hotel in New York some thirty-six hours later, dead tired.

The UN Security Council meeting went well, with no "nyet" for admission to membership of the UN for the Republic of Singapore and a no-dissenting vote for Singapore's UN membership at the General Assembly as well. But at the very moment of the formal admission to membership of the UN for the Republic of Singapore, a member of the Malaysian Permanent Representative Ramani's team at his representative office in New York came rushing up to me to inform me I was urgently required on a UN house phone in connection with some flight bookings for the mission on from New York and beyond. I therefore immediately went to the phone to take the call and attend to what required attending to and hence missed that historic event of admission of the Republic of Singapore to membership of the UN for which I had so dutifully planned and had hoped so much to personally observe. From the UN and New York, the mission first went to London and called on the Commonwealth & Foreign Office while I also had to settle several flight and hotel bookings for the mission through BOAC HQ. On then on BOAC to Nairobi in Kenya to start the first leg of the goodwill mission to Africa and the Middle East, Eastern Europe, South Asia, Southeast Asia and home.

In Nairobi, the delegation was very well received and had audiences with President Jomo Kenyatta and Vice President Oginga Odinga, and had the good fortune to meet Attorney General Tom Mboya at a reception, who struck me as a most wise and reasonable soul with very good charisma but who most unfortunately was assassinated not too long after. The British High Commissioner to East Africa, Sir Malcolm MacDonald, who had been in Singapore not too long before as British Commissioner to Southeast Asia and was known, at least by name if not more, to both DPM Dr Toh and Foreign Minister S Rajatnam, also met our delegation in Nairobi and most courteously even arranged for a day's safari ride through the nature reserve alongside the highway from the airport to the city which, most unfortunately, is really now far from what it used to be. Alex Josey, designated as the Foreign Minister's press liaison officer joined the delegation in London for the Africa leg and on from there to Yugoslavia and the USSR. Alex Josey had arrived from Palestine, around the time the state of Israel was recognised by the UN, in Malaya and Singapore with the British rulers around 1948 when the Emergency in Malaya was declared, to serve with the then British rulers in Malaya and Singapore, but had apparently proved too strident for some of those British rulers and been pushed out by them to become an independent press correspondent in Singapore. He was a good personal friend of the Foreign Minister who had called on his independent services from time to time. But, during the brief period of Singapore's existence as a state of Malaysia he had been ejected from Malaysia by the central government owing in no small part to his being Jewish, and retreated to London where a sister of his lived, and from where and when he had been invited by the Foreign Minister to join the delegation from London as a press liaison officer to Africa and on to Yugoslavia and the USSR. The Permanent Secretary to the Foreign Minister, who had been with the delegation from Singapore to New York, was left behind in New York by the delegation to become the Republic of Singapore's very first Permanent Representative to the UN in New York, which he was none too happy at all about as he was especially looking forward to going on the mission to Africa and on.

Others besides Alex Josey joined and departed the delegation along the way, including the DS (PMO) H F G Leembruggen, who joined the delegation in New York and on from there to London and Africa; and Abdul Rahim Ishak, the Political Secretary to the Minister for Culture, who joined the delegation in Nairobi, Kenya, and on from there all the way till our return to Singapore. Thus the delegation mirrored the diversity of the general population of the Republic of Singapore with representatives from the Chinese, Indian, Malay and even that most minor of minorities officially classified as "Others", the Eurasians, of whom there were two in that delegation, H F G Leembruggen and I and, although not really of and from Singapore, the delegation even had Jewish representation in the person of Alex Josey.

On from Nairobi in Kenya to Dar-es-Salaam in Tanzania where the delegation was treated to independence day celebrations in a stadium where the President of Tanzania and topmost representative from Zanzibar jointly poured sand from each of the former territories of Tanganyika and Zanzibar out of a large flagon onto the ground of the stadium to represent the recent amicable and peaceful incorporation of Zanzibar into Tanganyika to form Tanzania. Later, at a hall near the stadium to which the delegation retreated for a national day reception, members of the delegation got whispered news of the momentous ouster of Sukarno as President of Indonesia and hints of more to come. That reception suddenly became a test of patience and self-control for the Singapore delegation who desperately sought more reliable information and some confirmation at least of what was happening in Indonesia, Singapore's big neighbour. The delegation did however survive that ordeal and moved on according to plan and itinerary, owing to the pre-booked flights and accommodation for the remaining itinerary of our official programme, though our hearts were heavy and brows furrowed with anxiety and apprehension as to what the future might hold for our still-in-the-cradle new Republic of Singapore, neighbouring the now much disturbed giant Indonesia.

While in Lusaka, Zambia, the hapless and forlorn delegation members searched high and low and scrounged from wherever and whenever they could including the sorely missed Radio Karat, which they then could not find, for whatever information they could possibly glean, even from desperate rumours then floating around like flotsam and jetsam in the tide, that might possibly help them learn what had really happened to Sukarno himself and to the giant archipelagic Republic of Indonesia entity and might possibly befall, in consequence, new babe UN member little island Republic of Singapore from fallout of such an eruption.

Lusaka itself was so pleasant and relaxing and seemingly peaceful in that cool and far from humid Singapore as to lull the delegation into an euphoria that all might well be well in the world including that part of the world they had started out from seemingly such a long time ago. The official visits and calls too in Lusaka had, they thought, gone well and the only bother to bother them then was when what the delegation had thought was a most polite and innocuous of requests to our gentle and welcoming hosts to squeeze in a possible half day's visit to the famed world wonder of Victoria Falls to only the Zambian side and not also to the then Rhodesian was met with humming and hawing and side looks exchanged amongst our hosts that led on to frowns and a mumbled, "Let us check and get back to you!" Followed some time later with shakes of the heads, more frowns and then a very firm and final, "So sorry, yes, the view of Victoria Falls is best from the Zambian side as everyone knows and we do appreciate that and would like to share it with you; but unfortunately the Falls are much too far from where we are in Lusaka for even a day's let alone half day visit there. Come again, please, when you have more time!"

So on went the delegation then to Entebbe airport and Kampala, capital of Uganda. The delegation happened to be in time to be invited to an independence day celebration on the presidential palace grounds, following an independence day parade at which they were fortunate to witness a stunning fly-past of fighter jets. When our entourage arrived at the gates of the presidential palace for the garden reception, the huge iron gates to the grounds were tightly shut while a large and not-too-ruly crowd milled outside clamouring loundly to get in and the uniformed guards stood just within the securely closed gates. The guards shooed the milling crowd away to let our vehicular entourage through, then quickly swung the gates firmly shut with a loud clang, effectively closing the palace grounds off from that noisy and jostling crowd. While walking around the presidential palace grounds during the reception, I noticed a small group of young men in impeccable uniforms who did not seem to me to be Ugandan, talking animatedly amongst themselves in a language not quite known but not quite alien either to me. I later discovered it was Hebrew and that the small group of young men were from the Israeli Defence Force, on loan to the Uganda air force, and that they were in fact the pilots of that impressive fly-past we had witnessed a little earlier at the parade.

While in Kampala the delegation was most kindly treated to an excellent curry lunch at the home of the Indian Deputy High Commissioner who was then Acting High Commissioner in the absence of the Indian High Commissioner who was away. The curry lunch was cooked by the wife and cook from India of the Indian Deputy High Commissioner. My by then good friend Indian Deputy High Commissioner Thomas Abraham in Singapore had most kindly himself written to his own good friend the Indian High Commissioner in Lusaka, and also to others, to notify them of our delegation's visits and imploring them to "take very good care" of us during our brief stays.

Expecting to be away from Lusaka himself at the time of our visit the Indian High Commissioner had implored his Deputy to "take very good care" of us in Lusaka in his absence. Hence that excellent curry lunch at the home of the Indian Deputy High Commissioner then Acting Indian High Commissioner.

An added not-to-be-missed, once-in-a-lifetime treat that lunch was after the invitation by our host the Acting High Commissioner of India for coffee and brandy or other digestive on the balcony of the home of the Indian Deputy High Commissioner which commanded a beautiful and wondrous view of the great Lake Victoria. That was a real treat in itself!

From Kampala through Entebbe, it was on to Blantyre in Malawi. The official state guest house in Blantyre where we were to be accommodated as state guests was then occupied by another visiting delegation, so on our first night we stayed at the Kuchewa Inn not too far away. The Inn was owned and managed by an English couple who were long-time residents of Malawi from when it was still Nyasaland. It was accessed by a single winding road up a mountainside, along both sides of which road were lovely mature Jacaranda trees in beautiful full bloom. The fallen blossoms carpeted the road up that mountainside to our comfortable and quaint little Inn. That night I could hear loud coughing from outside the room, through the night-darkened window and curtains of my room. I discovered next morning it was from official security guards provided by our Malawi government hosts for the DPM and Foreign Minister. They had stood on guard the whole night under the trees in the grounds, each protected from the chilly night mountain air by nothing more than their simple plain light mufti clothing and a large light blanket each thrown over their shoulders.

The next day, we were able to move into the state guest house, a single storey bungalow standing on large grassy grounds, enclosed by a thick, tall and green hedge with a central iron gate guarded by uniformed personnel for access and egress.

From Blantyre we went back to Nairobi and on from there to Cairo via Kano in Nigeria where, during our transit, a Nigerian uniformed personnel quietly and unobtrusively boarded our aircraft, plonked himself down in one of the few empty seats, and adamantly refused to budge even when our airline crew tried to shoo him away. So off we flew to Cairo with him onboard. When we got to Cairo he quietly and quickly disembarked to disappear from sight and to where I knew not.

Our delegation was very well received in Cairo, in light mostly I thought of the earlier introductory personal letter of our PM to President Nasser himself. We stayed at the old Semi Ramis Hotel on a bank of the River Nile, owing to its having been specially recommended by Alex Josey based on his stay in Cairo in his earlier incarnation as a correspondent there not too long after World War II. Our Egyptian official handlers asked in surprise why we had not booked into the Hilton Hotel instead, also on a bank of the River Nile, but much newer and better according to our newfound Egyptian friends. This led to DPM Dr Toh admonishing me later in the semi-privacy of breakfast at our hotel the next day for being "So damn stupid again!" To which I gave a sheepish grin and answered, "Sorry, DPM!"

Alex Josey later took me on our own private visits the next day, around Cairo to some of the places he used to haunt in his previous life there, including the Cairo Tower. On another occasion I took a taxi by myself to mail some material acquired along our itinerary back to MFA Singapore. When I asked the taxi driver at the end the ride for the fare he answered in fluent English, "By the meter

…", and quoted me an exorbitant price in Egyptian pounds. I quickly looked at the meter myself and retorted back in English, "No, that's not correct, by the meter it should only be …" stating the correct fare by the meter. The taxi driver gave a big guffaw and said, "Oh you can read Arabic … OK pay me that then!" That was one time I was glad I had indeed paid good heed to the PM's early advice to me to be diligent and put a little effort into passing Jawi for my Malay Standard II examination for confirmation in my appointment. It had taught me to read the Jawi and Arabic numerals that enabled me to quote the correct fare by the meter to that enterprising taxi driver.

From Cairo we went on to Tunis in Tunisia where we had an uneventful visit except for a little diversion in the coffee shop of our hotel one afternoon after lunch while waiting to be picked up for our next appointment. The DPM, being adventuresome, ordered a cup of Turkish coffee, which he had never drunk before. When the orders arrived at our small and low coffee table, he said, "What a small, stupid-looking cup of coffee." Then he gulped it all down in one go, coffee grounds and all, before anyone could stop him, and immdiately spluttered the coffee all over the coffee table and over those seated near him, followed by the coffee grounds, very sheepishly and most apologetically. On another occasion, when we had some free time, Leembruggen invited me to join him for an excursion to the Kasbah to shop for some curios and souvenirs. We walked to a small shop in the Kasbah where the Indian shop assistant standing outside invited us in, saying in fluent English, "You're from the Singapore delegation, no?" He probably recognised us from press reports and photos of the Singapore delegation's visit to Tunis. "Come in, make yourselves welcome. Stay as long as you wish, buy as much as you want. And don't worry about having to carry whatever you buy back to Singapore in your baggage or about payment in Tunisian money or US dollars. We can arrange to deliver whatever you buy to Singapore and you can collect it when you get home from an address in Singapore I will give you. You can also make payment there in your own Singapore dollars." Both Leembruggen and I were very surprised, but we did buy a few curios and souvenirs each. Leembruggen, who returned to Singapore earlier, and I went separately following our respective returns to Singapore to the address given, which turned out to be an Indian-owned store on High Street, to collect our individual orders, which were both received in good order and complete, and paid for on collection in Singapore dollars. There was no fuss nor any hassle at all. That was a very good lesson for both Leembruggen and I in how the informal international business and trade network of Indian-owned and managed small enterprises operated.

After Tunis our delegation went on to Algiers in Algeria. Ahmed Ben Bella, a good friend of our PM, was no more in power but our delegation was very well received by his successors in Algeria and made to feel most welcome. It was a pleasant but uneventful visit after which we were glad to fly on by Air France to Paris and a most welcome short break while the DPM and Foreign Minister S Rajaratnam made an official call on the French foreign relations department at Quai d'Orsay. From Paris our main delegation flew on to Belgrade in then Yugoslavia, while Leembruggen returned from Paris to Singapore via London.

It was for me a most eye-opening and interesting visit to Belgrade. We were very well received at the very highest levels, and it was also a good introduction for what was to come, on the next leg of our visit, in Moscow. Where it was, not entirely by happenstance, the time of the annual October Revolution celebrations. While in Belgrade, I was surprised to see donkey carts still trundling the streets and tractors clanking their slow way beside them as well.

During a short break in our official programme one afternoon, the Political Secretary, who had joined us in Nairobi, invited me to join him to meet an old businessman friend of his from Singapore, who was then in Belgrade on a business trip. Learning our delegation would be in Belgrade then he had likely planned to be there too at the time, and at that hotel. He had phoned the Political Secretary to make an appointment to pay an informal courtesy call. We met in the hotel's main lounge over Yugoslavian brandy touched with soda, plates of cubed goats' cheese, dried apple slices, and pickled onion as well. A delectable combination.

While in the lounge chatting and savouring our brandy sodas and titbits, the Political Secretary casually remarked on the well-dressed and attractive young women who were gathered at different tables in the main lounge in threes or fours, sipping on glasses of what looked like plain soda water and doing little else except chatting and laughing. The businessman friend responded that he understood, though was not able himself to confirm, that those young women were waiting for possible assignations arranged through select members of the hotel staff. He understood that most, if not all, would be only too willing to go to bed with guests at the hotel or elsewhere for a few US dollars and a pair or two of nylons or bars of Swiss chocolate. A sign, declared that Singapore businessman, of the intrusion into the former strict moral code and standards of behaviour of a Socialist Yugoslavia, of decadent capitalism.

We were most warmly welcomed in Moscow by our Russian hosts, if not by the weather which had begun to get cold and even to snow. Sergei Severin, the Russian TASS correspondent who was previously based in Bangkok and had recently transferred to Singapore, was amongst our Russian hosts to welcome us to Moscow and the USSR and accompany us on lesser official calls and visits. There were the usual mandatory visits to and calls at the Kremlin and attendance at the grand and most impressive October Revolution Parade in Red Square and at the Moscow Circus, Bolshoi Ballet and an October Revolution grand concert at which military-looking young men belted out solo or in choir, what we were told were patriotic, but sounded to us very military, songs in Russian. Later, we each found an album, in our hotel rooms, of several 78 rpm records of those songs by those singers waiting for us. Our hotel itself was old with dismal and dark corridors where we often feared ghosts of the spiritual and human kind might lurk in the dark. On level one, by the main entrance, there was a small room the door to which was always kept shut, while plain-clothed unknown characters often slunk silently in or out. One day as I was going past that door, after entering the hotel through its main entrance, I encountered a man leaving the room who spoke to me in what by then I guessed must be Russian. I just shook my head, smiled and said, "Nyet," then walked on past to my room. He got most upset and let out a blistering torrent in Russian after me. Another time as I left my room for breakfast, an old Russian woman dressed in a simple plain white uniform, whom I presumed to be from housekeeping, spoke to me in Russian. I just shook my head, smiled, said "Nyet," and walked on to her utter disgust and dismay, which showed very obviously on her face. When we got back to Singapore following completion of that entire trip, the DPM gave a speech to a cheering crowd assembled at Paya Lebar Airport to welcome us home, and spoke of a member of his delegation, "Hochstadt" by name, who looked so much like a Russian that even Russians in Moscow spoke to him in Russian, to the great delight of that assembled wildly cheering and welcoming crowd.

The flight out from Moscow to New Delhi was on Aeroflot, with a transit stop in the dark at Tashkent for refuelling. I shared a first-class cabin on that Aeroflot flight with the Foreign Minister. We had a full-sized bunk each, with a curtain that could be drawn to close off each bunk. The stout middle-aged senior Aeroflot flight attendant assigned to take charge of our cabin came just once before we took off, to announce we should fasten our seat belts, then disappeared. We only saw her again as we were about to land at New Delhi when she appeared with a big steaming mug of black coffee for each of us, then disappeared again. I was later told by one of our hosts in New Delhi that that was quite normal and to be expected as, in a socialist state such as the USSR, the concept of service was quite foreign. It was a very interesting visit to New Delhi. But by then we ourselves and our clothes were beginning to show obvious signs of the wear and tear to be expected from nearly two months' continuous travel out of a single suitcase each. At a dinner hosted by PM Indira Gandhi, I was seated at the table a couple of seats away from her, while the DPM was seated immediately in front of her and the Foreign Minister was on her immediate right. I happened to notice, while taking my seat at the dinner table that the zip on my trousers had quite apparently given up the ghost and and grip to securely hold the opening of my trousers together. So I quickly and unobtrusively tucked my large white table napkin into the top of my pants to cover the gaping zipper as a small apron would. Indira Gandhi got up during the dinner to propose a toast and everyone else followed. I did so too with my large white table napkin tucked securely into the top of my trousers, hanging over like the apron it was then supposed to be. In the course of that toast I spied a distraught DPM, out a corner of my eye, surreptitiously waving and pointing desperately trying to signal me. I pretended not to notice. Later, when we were back at our hotel, the DPM gave me a tongue-lashing. I said, "Sorry DPM, the zip on my trousers gave way, from some two months' continuous hard wear and tear. I thought it best to cover myself in that manner, to save both PM Indira Gandhi and myself from any embarrassment." The DPM immediately shut up, did not say more, but waved his right hand madly to dismiss me. I immediately complied most happily and readily.

Rangoon was an experience in itself. We stayed at the Russian-built and state-owned Inya Lake Hotel. One day when we had a break in our official programme the Political Secretary borrowed a small rowboat from the boatshed nearby and asked me to go with him for a row on the lake by the hotel. We were none too experienced or strong rowers and found it difficult, after we were quite far out on the lake, to get back to the pier against the strong current and wind. We had to get a tow back to the pier from a couple of university students out for an evening's row themselves in another small rowboat. On another excursion, we visited the glittering-gold Shwedagon Pagoda, a truly unforgettable experience.

We were welcomed to Phnom Penh by Prince Sihanouk himself and housed in a royal guest house as state guests. One day another member of our delegation and I went on a foray to the main general post office to send off some official and personal mail, then to the main marketplace for a little shopping. An official car and driver sent us to the general post office and on to the marketplace, where we dismissed the car and driver as we did not want to keep both too long. After shopping, we hailed a pedicab for the ride back to our royal guest house, where the two sentries on guard at the main gate were most amused to see two official state guests roll up at the main gate in a for-hire pedicab. They denied our pedicab entry through the main front gate of that royal guest house, not that our pedicab driver himself dared to venture into the grounds of that royal guest house with his two foreign-looking passengers.

We made a side trip from Phnom Penh to Angkor Wat and stayed in a hotel there for a night, during which we were treated to a special moonlight performance, on the wide main causeway across the moat, by Prince Sihanouk's Royal Ballet. A day's excursion around the main temple ruins was a special treat for us the next day.

From Phnom Penh we flew to Bangkok from where the Foreign Minister, after a brief transit in Bangkok, flew with his PA to Colombo, on a side trip and official visit to Ceylon. Before he left, he asked for an official gift from the stock I had purchased in Singapore and carried on the trip for the DPM and Foreign Minister to present along the way. I had estimated the total number of gifts we would need and had got that number, plus a few extra, with the remaining last two specially reserved for DPM to present to PM Thanom Kittikachorn and his Deputy. I had not taken into account any official gift the Foreign Minister might need to present on his side visit to Ceylon, so I got a car and driver from Pitsanoluke Palace, where our Thai hosts had put us up, and drove together with the PA to the DPM to Chinatown, where were the only shops open on a Sunday then in Bangkok. I found the selection of possible gifts was not quite right but had no choice and could only hope the best choice the DPM's PA and I could make from what was available would do. In the event, very possibly our Thai hosts were too polite to make any complaint or caustic remark about an official gift that was so obviously of local origin.

From Bangkok it was back to Singapore and home. Most welcome to me after over two months' continuous travel, living out of a single suitcase and with just two suits: one to wear in all seasons and for all occasions, while the other was in dry cleaning wherever and whenever possible along that long, long road that led back to Singapore. In those days, especially in Africa, same-day dry cleaning was often not available, so often the same not-too-clean and often dishevelled suit had to be worn over and over again. Even if it did not look too clean, the hope always was that it would not smell bad. While the DPM was on the temporary stage at Paya Lebar Airport beside the parking tarmac, addressing the assembled crowd, I sought refuge in the VIP room, only to find the former Finance Minister and recently appointed Minister of Defence there already having a quiet cool drink. The Minister guffawed loudly when he saw me and announced, "You're coming to my Ministry! Ha! Ha! Ha! You're coming to my Ministry! Ha! Ha! Ha!" He would not then say more, but kept chuckling merrily to himself. I later learnt from my brother-in-law, Derrick, then OC Security, who had got it from a security officer of his who had overheard, while I was away, that the Minister of Defence had sought to get me posted to his newly set up Ministry of the Interior & Defence to head his Manpower Division. However, the PM had already agreed, to the surprise and chargrin of the Minister of Defence, to my being assigned, following Separation, to serve on special assignment as Administrative Secretary to the delegation to the UN in New York and onwards and, on return to Singapore from that trip, to go on posting to the newly established Foreign Ministry to help get it up and going. Apparently the Defence Minister then reminded the PM that he had agreed to loan me to the PM as his Secretary, on special assignment pre-general election and establishment of Malaysia, and had expected I would subsequently be returned to his charge for reposting. The PM apparently then agreed to the request of the Minister of Defence to my posting to the newly established Ministry of Interior & Defence, under Minister of Defence Dr Goh Keng Swee. However, following our return from that two-month sojourn, the toenail of the big toe on my right foot which could not be adequately attended to on that long and gruelling trip but had troubled me a lot, was found by my GP upon my return to have become ingrown and was about to turn septic. He advised I should go into Mount Alvernia Hospital the next day to undergo day surgery and excise the already infected toenail, which I did and was on medical leave after to rest and recuperate at home. Following which I reported to MID HQ for my new assignment, limping along with a slipper on my right foot. As a result, I missed the thank you dinner the DPM hosted for the returned delegation at Sri Temasek. Missing out too on the very fine film footage, shown for the first time, taken by our delegation's ever-cheerful cameraman, Mun Choor Seng, from then Radio & Television Singapore. He was also the most welcome supplier of good chilli sauce and sambal free of charge to us at our meals along the way, more than two months' continuous gruelling mission to New York and on, for which chilli sauce and sambal us members of the delegation remained ever grateful to Mun Chor Seng.

John Hochstadt and Rosa Delphina née D'Almeida.

Henry David Hochstadt and Beryl Lucy née Phillips on their wedding day.

The Hochstadt children. *Front row, left to right*: John Philip and Carl John; *middle row, left to right*: Cora Eleanor, Myrna Anita and Joan Carole; *back row*: hrh. Photo taken on the front steps leading to 14 Parkstone Road.

Left to right: Cora, Joan, Beryl, Henry, hrh and Myrna. Photo taken on 14 Parkstone Road lawn beside 6 Parkstone Road.

hrh BA(Honours) graduation 1958.

hrh and Peggy Wai Chee née Leong on their wedding day in 1960.

hrh as chairman of NOL.

hrh receiving the Public Administration Gold Medal from President Benjamin Sheares at the 1978 National Day awards. Source: The Straits Times © Singapore Press Holdings Limited. Reprinted with permission.

The 1982 "Budget Night" Dinner of MOF's Budget Division. *Seated, left to right*: Dileep Nair and Sim Cheng Tee Henry; *standing, left to right*: Huan Tzu Hong, Low Ah Tee, hrh, Tan Khay Quee and Ajith Prasad.

hrh gives a speech at the farewell and appreciation dinner in his honour, given by MOE HQ staff, principals of junior colleges, secondary and primary schools at Shangri-La Hotel, 15 May 1980.

Lunch in Shanghai following the launch of a Neptune Orient Lines ship at Jiangnan Shipyard, Shanghai.

hrh and Peggy Wai Chee at the Great Wall of China following the NOL launch at Jiangnan Shipyard.

hrh with President Nelson Mandela of Republic of South Africa following the presentation of credentials by hrh as first High Commissioner for Republic of Singapore to Republic of South Africa.

hrh in the latter years of corporate life.

IX

Ministry of Interior & Defence

The MID HQ was at Pearl's Hill, which also housed the Police HQ and the Police Radio Division. I spent a few weeks in the Home Affairs Division, hanging around with not much really to do, after which, one day for no apparent reason at all, I was summarily summoned to the office of Perm Sec (MID) and told I was to report "with immediate effect" to the Manpower Division (MP Div) and take over as Director (Manpower) or DMP. This was in fact the position the Minister of Defence had mentioned when he told me I would be going to MID for, all those weeks before at Paya Lebar Airport on return of the delegation to the UN in New York and on. I was later given to understand that objections had been raised by some of the more conservative military types at the core of MID HQ to a civilian such as I with no military experience, becoming DMP and lording it over the uniformed military establishment. However, there had been a near riot at Shenton Way Camp, during a recruitment for fresh regulars when several unemployed youths who had been waiting there for hours to be enlisted were bluntly ordered to leave and were told there was no place for them in the military establishment. The order then came from the Minister himself that he had specially asked for me to be posted to MID to take over as DMP and I should take over forthwith. So there I was, a new babe, first civilian DMP.

It was indeed a near Herculean task to get that Manpower Division up and going. Almost from scratch with, to begin, just my brand new civilian PA, Katherine Khoo; a civilian assistant from the Administrative Service, Leo Lian Lim, who had worked with me previously in the Finance Ministry and with whom I had dealings later when he was posted to the People's Association and I was Secretary to PM; and a mobilised Singapore Volunteer Corps (SVC) officer au fait with army manpower protocol, then Captain G Arumugam. They made an invaluable team to get us going on the path forward to a then far from clear goal in those confused and troubled early days of MID. Our first task was defined as building up the ranks of the regular army personnel. Before our Central Manpower Base (CMPB) recommended by the MID advisors, the "Mexicans", based on their own experience, could be set up and going on the grounds of the old Kallang Airport where the Peoples' Association had its HQ, and National Service came on stream, our small band of hardcore MP Div staff had to go themselves, besides sending dependable and trusted assistants from amongst mobilised former SVC personnel and police officers on secondment, out to the field to try to recruit the regulars needed then to build up the Singapore Armed Forces (SAF) from near zero. They went first to the Community Centres, to select those who had voluntarily come forth, but later found that far too many of those selected from amongst that number, who had been asked to report later to designated centres to be sworn in and signed on and taken to their camps, just failed to appear. This was attributed to a traditional disdain among the more conservative and traditional Chinese, who regarded service in the army as amongst the lowest forms of service for any young man from a decent family.

It was found that, when any such potential recruit got home and reported to his family that he had just signed on for service in the army, his mother, grandmother, sisters and other female kin, would be dismayed and bemoan the fact, then desperately seek to prevent or dissuade that potential recruit to the SAF from persisting in his folly. My MP Div eager beaver, bright young boys, then devised a cunning new plan: they would arrange for some fresh young civilian magistrates only too eager to get out of their stuffy offices to be taken to the designated Community Centres, so they could quickly swear in the selected youth there on the spot, who could then be transported immediately in army trucks bearing "MID" registration plates to the camps. However, it was only too soon discovered those new recruits would invariably not be properly dressed nor equipped for immediate life as new SAF recruits, while some would have left loved ones or others, waiting at the Community Centres for their dear sons, grandsons, brothers or whomsoever to return to their bosoms.

The Singapore Armed Forces Training Institute (SAFTI), set up around that time, brought on its own set of problems and headaches for MP Div and, of course, DMP in turn. Experienced and good regular non-commissioned officers (NCOs) in the SAF had to be found, and urgently, to serve as trainers and models for those new recruits to be trained as future NCOs and officers, and the more seasoned regulars and mobilised volunteers, including a couple of regular senior police officers on secondment to SAF had to be roped in for the task. For SAFTI's required complement of such for its Section Leaders' training courses. Ever resourceful Captain Arumugam recommended a few such NCOs from 1st Battalion, Singapore Infantry Regiment (1SIR) whom he knew or had heard of for immediate posting to SAFTI. Very soon after the posting orders had gone out I was peremptorily summoned to the office of the Director (General Staff), or DGS, to be confronted there by the DGS himself and the commanding officer (CO) of 1SIR, a Colonel on loan to SAF from the British army. The Colonel complained bitterly to the DGS of my ill-conceived posting of his most experienced and best NCOs to SAFTI, depriving his unit of essential personnel to adequately carry out its regular role and, he stressed, its internal security role as and when needed. The DGS, who himself was a very senior police officer on secondment to MID and very much aware of the internal security role, stood firmly behind his CO, backing him up fully and giving me a blistering tongue lashing in front of the CO, no doubt for the latter's benefit. I could merely respond limply that I had been expressly instructed to give top priority to SAFTI's needs, but had already begun to believe that everything in and for SAF was "top priority". So, if the DGS himself considered 1SIR's needs more "top priority" than SAFTI's at that point of time, so be it. Who was I, a mere civilian DMP, to argue about operational needs with the DGS himself. And we left it at that. But, of course, the problem for MP Div and DMP of finding the right personnel, or even those who might be just barely suitable, for SAFTI remained. It took much time and effort and, of course, deviousness too to salve, even if not really solve, that problem. And the several other such problems that constantly prickled the MPD then.

I recall the Director (Logistics), a good friend who had worked with me when I was Secretary to the PM and he was in the People's Association, complaining to me in the privacy of my office about his difficulty in acquiring arms, ammunition and equipment for a developing SAF, Republic of Singapore Navy (RSN) and Republic of Singapore Airforce (RSAF). And bemoaning the fact that, even with the money, it often required persuasion and the right connections to get such needs even barely satisfied. I told him his Division's problems were nowhere near comparable to those of my Division. As, even with the money, MP Div had not only to try to persuade the productive men and women of Singapore to produce the young men needed for a developing SAF, RSN and RSAF, but would then have to wait some eighteen years at least for the fruit of such persuasion to mature into the young recruits and potential NCOs and officers needed by SAF immediately, let alone those we would need in the future. Everything in MID was needed quick-quick, but MPD needed time to deliver which was never forthcoming. My good friend Director (Logistics), gave a sheepish smile and kept quiet.

Another problem that SAFTI encountered in those early days was that the promotion efforts to secure the first recruits for SAFTI had been oversold. Within their first few weeks, a significant number of trainees sought to drop out and asked to be allowed to quit. Owing, it seemed, to disappointment due to their expectations over the overall training programme itself and to its being far too vigorous and strenuous for them. The programme had been largely devised and strongly recommended by the "Mexican" advisors based on their own experience. An urgent meeting was convened at SAFTI of all the recruits then in training, chaired by the Perm Sec (MID), with the DGS, DMP and Director (SAFTI) in attendance by order. The Perm Sec (MID) gave the recruits a good talking too, while exhorting them to continue and do their best in their own interest and for the nation that needed them then and would more so following completion of their training to be the officers and NCOs of the nation for the foreseeable future. It seemed to do the trick. SAFTI's very first Section Leaders' course was completed with minimal dropouts along the tough and bruising way.

Compulsory National Service (NS) was brought into effect for all Singapore men deemed fit enough from eighteen years of age, initially for of two and a half years for those selected after the Section Leaders' course to go on for the officers' course, and two years for the others. It was decided the National Service Ordinance, which became law in the 1950s, should be amended and brought up to date rather than repealed and replaced by a brand-new law. That was done and a smart move it was. The CMPB, then at Kallang, was to be the central base for induction of the very first recruits into NS. Director CMPB arranged for me and my team from MID HQ to be shown around before the VIP tour for the Minister, Perm Sec and others. During my team's tour, a cameraman from the Ministry of Culture, who was a Chinese middle school graduate whom I had first befriended on those Sunday Constituency Tours while I was Secretary to the PM, came up to me and quietly insisted, through hand signals and a mixture of Mandarin and English words, that the signs CMPB intended to use for the new induction into NS should be shown to us. I so ordered. On immediate sight of those signs, the cameraman shook his head and effectively conveyed to me that none of those signs would do and should all be disposed of and destroyed. He manged to convey, with the help of some interpretation, that those very signs had in fact been the ones used for the NS drive of the 1950s under British rule and the old unamended NS law. The Chinese characters used in those signs were at the very core of what had triggered the middle school students' violent objection then to National Service. I immediately ordered those old signs be destroyed, and fresh signs be made strictly following the Chinese characters that the Ministry of Culture cameraman had so kindly and helpfully written for me on a blank page of his notebook. I was most grateful to that cameraman from the Ministry of Culture who had been a regular on the PM's Sunday Constituency Tours in the early 1960s who had high regard and great respect for PM Lee Kuan Yew.

Not too long after, there was a change of Minister of Defence, with Goh Keng Swee going over to the Finance Ministry and the then Finance Minister, Lim Kim San, taking over as Minister of Defence. Meanwhile, a former boss of mine at the Finance Ministry who had been retired under Malayanisation, Tony Colton, and was at the time personnel manager at *The Straits Times*, asked me to join him for tea one afternoon at what I discovered would be at the home of his big boss only after I had accepted the invitation. His big boss lived off Nassim Road in a prime residential district of Singapore. During this tea I was offered Colton's job so he could move on to some other managerial position in The Straits Times Group. Colton had met me alone a couple of times before that, having first called on me unannounced one evening while my wife Peggy and I were settling into our new house at Sunset View in Clementi Park. I agreed to accept the job, on no immediately better salary or terms as I then enjoyed in the civil service, on probation for three months during which either party could end the employment contract with twenty-four hours' notice, no questions asked. I tendered the required one month's notice for my resignation from MID, during which the new Minister of Defence and other senior officers of MID tried with no success to persuade me to reconsider. The time soon came for me to leave MID, I was given a thank you note and rather boisterous farewell dinner at a small but good Chinese restaurant near MID HQ by several fellow officers in MID HQ and a few others from the SAF units including, of course, CMPB. I then found myself in a small office at *The Straits Times*, then off River Valley Road at its junction with Kim Seng Road. My office was beside Tony Colton's, whom I was to understudy during my probation. I had been there for just one week plus the public holiday for Deepavali when I got a call from the then PA to the PM, A Sankaran, whom I had got to know quite well and taken a liking to, as a friend. He had been introduced to me by my good press officer friend, K R S Vas, over drinks at a small grog shop on the upper floor of an old shophouse on Hallpike Street, opposite the entrance to the then Attorney General's Chambers off High Street hence our code name for that drinking hole, "AG's Chambers". Sankaran told me, in his very calm manner, that "the boss" wanted to see me. I asked why and when, and Sankaran answered, "You know why and you know when; you know the boss. When he says he wants to see someone, he means now, or even yesterday! Come!" So off I went to City Hall, as quick as I could. When I got there I was ushered right away, with no fuss at all, into the PM's office. He calmly greeted me and waved me to a seat before his customarily highly polished and completely bare desk. Then said, "When I got back from my official trip, the DPM who had been covering for me as PM, told me you had resigned and said that I should speak to you to get you to withdraw your resignation and come back to the service. Before I do, tell me honestly, are you really satisfied with what you're doing at *The Straits Times*, and find it interesting, compared to when you worked for me in the civil service?" I told the PM that, what I had been doing in his office as Secretary, and in the civil service had indeed been far more varied, interesting and satisfying, than my current job as personnel manager-to-be of *The Straits Times* would seem to offer. "Then come back! Quit *The Straits Times*, though I don't really know how you could do so speedily without penalty. But I don't think it would be best that you return to MID. You could come back to my office if you wish." I assured the PM it would be no problem for me to leave *The Straits Times* immediately; I was initially on probation for three months, during which either party only needed to provide twenty-four hours' notice with no reason required. As to where I should like to be posted, my preference was the Ministry of Foreign Affairs (MFA). In fact the PM himself had agreed to my posting to the MFA immediately following the mission to the UN in New York and on, but then Minister of Defence Dr Goh Keng Swee had got my posting to MFA diverted to MID. While in MID I had been for an interview at the Public Service Commission (PSC) for an MFA overseas posting, but that posting had been thwarted by Perm Sec (MID). The PM said nothing, picked up his phone from the wall cabinet behind him and said, "Raja, Hochstadt's now with me. He's coming back to service and will be in your Ministry. He'll report to your Permanent Secretary." He then dismissed me with a wave of his hand.

Back I went to *The Straits Times*, I reported what had transpired to Colton and told him I was, there and then, tendering the twenty-four hours' notice of my resignation as required under the terms of my three months' probation and that he should not expect me in office the next day. Colton remonstrated and tried to persuade me not to resign but I persisted and left. The next day I was in Perm Sec (MFA) Woon Wah Siang's office in City Hall. He asked what I would like to do in MFA and I told him I would like an overseas posting. I added that, when applications were first opened for the Foreign Service, I had applied then though I was already at MID. I had been selected by the Public Service Commission, and S T Stewart, former Perm Sec (PMO) and head of the civil service, had personally asked for me to be posted to Canberra as his number two, where he was to be posted himself as the very first High Commissioner for the Republic of Singapore. However, Perm Sec (MID) had then told me he had advised the PSC that the Minister of Defence had personally asked for me to be specially assigned to MID as DMP and the PSC immediately rescinded my posting to the MFA for service overseas. Woon called the MFA's head of admin, Balbir Singh, to his office and told him to settle with me in regard to my overseas posting. Balbir Singh asked me, after consulting some records, whether I would like to be posted to Washington as number two to the Ambassador. I told Balbir I would be prepared to, but needed to consult my wife first as she would have to get leave from the university where she was then an assistant librarian. Immediately, I conferred with my wife, Peggy, who said once the posting was confirmed she would seek leave without pay from her university library position so she and our little daughter Karen, then just six, could go on the posting with me. Balbir Singh then took action for the necessary higher approvals, which were forthcoming. But very soon there were unhappy rumblings from more established MFA personnel about the apparent jumping over heads by the "PM's blue-eyed boy" for a plum MFA overseas posting. The still rather new Ambassador to Washington was also very pointedly asked whether a Eurasian would be the right choice for posting to Washington as number two or, for that matter, even to the UN in New York. The Ambassador to Washington, being still new to the game of diplomacy was non-committal, but expressed the view it was probably safer not to, which led to my posting to Washington being withdrawn forthwith. Instead I was assigned to head the Admin & Consular Division of MFA. Peggy was most disappointed and told me she was glad she had not, by then, sought approval of the university for leave without pay and initiated action to rent out our still new home. We had earlier agreed that the house would eventually be registered in both our names, but initially it was solely in Peggy's name since the loan from the university would be on rather better terms than I could get under the government officers' housing loan scheme.

I headed the Admin & Consular Div of the MFA for about a year, and made official inspection visits to our missions in the region, before I was summoned to report for duty under my old boss, Tan Chok Kian, of the Establishment Branch in the Budget Division of the Finance Ministry. I later discovered that when the MFA got a message that I was to be posted to the Establishment Branch in the Budget Division of the Ministry of Finance, someone in upper echelons of the civil service of MFA, for reasons of his own, had quietly advised the Finance Minister he had best first seek approval of the PM as my posting to the MFA had been at the personal direction of the PM. I discovered the Finance Minister had then written to the PM to the effect that, though I was not outstanding, both the Establishment Branch in the Budget Division and the Economic Development Division of the Finance Ministry had requested for me. But the Finance Minister was more inclined to post me to the Establishment Branch where the Finance Minister thought I would be more useful. He intended to post me there should the PM have no objection. The PM replied, in quick time, that I had myself asked to be posted to MFA and, if I wished now to be posted to the Establishment Branch in the Budget Division of the Finance Ministry, so be it, the PM would have no objection. And so it came to be.

Before I left MFA, however, I saw another general election through in 1968 as Assistant Group Returning Officer. An interesting experience for me, as was the earlier general election of 1963 just before Malaysia.

X

Ministry of Finance: First Homecoming

My return to the Establishment (Estab) Branch of the Budget Division of the Ministry of Finance (MOF) was a homecoming to where I had begun my civil service career in 1959. Even to being back at level five of the Fullerton Building, where I was in 1962 and from when and where I began my travels within and for the civil service. Furthermore my immediate boss in Estab was once again Tan Chok Kian, who had been my immediate boss from 1959 to 1962 when I was first in the civil service and at MOF. But the big boss had changed to Lee Keng Tuan, then Acting Perm Sec (Finance) (Budget). He had been in Estab earlier as Deputy Secretary (Service Conditions) when I was there, though he was not my immediate boss then. However, Lee Keng Tuan left not too long after on loan to the Asian Development Bank in Manila, Philippines. Tan Chok Kian then became Acting Perm Sec (Budget). All in, out of my thirty years in the civil service, I spent eleven altogether in MOF.

The Estab Branch of MOF's Budget Division in 1969 was quite a different animal, one much more tame and settled, compared to the one I had left in 1962 to go on special assignment to PM's office.

Though I did have my very first experience in the later posting of representing the government in the Industrial Arbitration Court (IAC) in a case involving daily-rated employees, many of whom had been absorbed from the former City Council. It was the very first such IAC case, so there were no precedents to follow nor to guide. The Public Daily-Rated Employees' Union Federation, comprising mainly those daily-rated employees who came from the former Municipal Council, led by old union foe Suppiah, had been fighting very hard regarding matters under contention hanging over from the former Public Utilities Board (PUB). But Suppiah and his supporters were frustrated when the case was unilaterally referred by the government under the law to the IAC to be heard, meaning that no further industrial action could by law be mounted by the unions. The union was represented in that case before the IAC by Member of Parliament-cum-trade unionist, N Govindasamy, a good friend of mine, who, most unfortunately did not live too much longer thereafter. But not owing to that IAC case nor what immediately followed. The case did not go through to the bitter end in the IAC. It was taken out of the IAC by order of the government, owing to what was thought to have been external influence and pressure brought to bear on the IAC and that case. It was referred then to a special committee to determine and decide. I found it very tough representing the government owing to it being my very first case before the IAC with no precedence to follow nor to guide. I did find it interesting, nevertheless. It reminded me of the old wild and untamed days of Estab and the far from tame and amenable trade unions and trade unionists we had to work with to try to reach settlement or to bring strenuously to heel.

In 1972, Singapore Airlines (SIA) was just established, arising from the split, following Separation, of Malaysia-Singapore Airlines (MSA) which it was part of in its transitional life from the original Malayan

Airways Ltd (MAL). I was informed through the grapevine, or in SAF parlance, what was commonly referred to as "Radio Karat" or "Rusty Wireless", that SIA was looking for a personnel manager to take over from its long-time personnel manager inherited from MAL. And I was persuaded to apply. The then personnel manager was known to me personally having been my senior at St Andrew's School. I was told he wished to move on to some other job in the airline but could do so only if he found someone acceptable to take over from him. I was acceptable or found to be so. But before I could take on the appointment, I had to get my release from MOF. I dutifully sought my release. My big boss in the MOF then, Tan Chok Kian, the Acting Perm Sec (Finance) (Budget), called me to his office and gave me a stern talking to, ending in no uncertain terms: "No way!"

Not long after, Perm Sec (Finance) (Economic Development), George Edwin Bogaars who had been Perm Sec (MID) during my time in MID and with whom I then had some lesser differences but had made up and been on very good terms with since, called me to his office, also in the Fullerton Building, one day for a friendly chat over a cup of coffee. He then, in his capacity as head of the civil service and Perm Sec (Finance) (Economic Development), offered to recommend me for appointment, if I so desired, as non-executive director on the board of SIA and, pending SIA becoming operational, appointed also meanwhile, from the Singapore side, as an alternate director of MSA. He asked, too, if I might in addition desire to be appointed to the Board of Neptune Orient Lines (NOL), the state-owned shipping line. I answered, "Yes," to both with no hesitation at all. It struck me then that it would be a good idea to be on the boards of the state-owned international air and sea carriers. Bogaars kept his word. I was soon non-executive director on the boards of both NOL and SIA, and, meanwhile, an alternate director of MSA. Bogaars had the wherewithal then to make such recommendations and have them fulfilled, no doubt owing to his concurrent appointments as head of the civil service and member of the then government Directorships Consultancy & Appointments Council.

George Bogaars was also largely instrumental in getting me nominated as our civil service representative to several regional conferences of the UN Economic & Social Commission for Asia and the Pacific (ESCAP) in Bangkok. In addition he got me nominated to one such conference held at the US State Department in Washington DC. He seemed all-powerful to me then and only too willing and ready to make amends for differences we had in MID that he thought I still held against him, but which I had just about forgotten all about by then. I was most appreciative and ever grateful to George Edwin Bogaars. Around that time too, before he went away to the US for several months on a US award, he recommended me to cover for him in his absence as Acting Perm Sec (Finance) (Economic Development), which I enjoyed immensely. Though my good friend Haider Sithawalla, who was in the Economic Development Division, complained bitterly then, and still does, that as Acting Perm Sec (Finance) (Economic Development) I had the gall to sneakily, behind his back, check his office files to see if he had indeed done what he was supposed to do and said he had done. But we are still good personal friends and have been since we were contemporary undergraduates in the old University of Malaya at Bukit Timah. My time at the MOF soon came to an end when, in 1972, I was told I had to move on to the Ministry of Communication to take over from Ngiam Tong Dow, who had himself recommended me to replace him. Ngiam Tong Dow had been a classmate of Haider's in the University of Malaya at Bukit Timah and a good friend of Haider's and mine from those days. Following posting to the Ministry of Communication, I was not to get back to the MOF again till my final stint there from 1981, following a year and a half secondment on special assignment to the Monetary Authority of Singapore (MAS).

XI

Ministry of Communication

Life in the Ministry of Communication (Min Comm), 1972–1975, was much more complicated and tougher than in my previous posting: my first MOF homecoming. For one, there were only some half a dozen senior officers in the Ministry HQ, which had direct responsibility then over road transport including the Registry of Vehicles and overall responsibility over the Department of Civil Aviation, Marine Department and Postal Department, with statutory appendages, the Port of Singapore Authority, which was a large organisation, and the Singapore Telephone Board, which was itself merged with the Telecommunication Authority of Singapore. Small head, relatively small body and several, rather than just a pair of each, huge arms and legs. The immediate big problem of Min Comm then was road transport, particularly the public bus services. The Singapore Traction Company (STC) had been set up and initially owned solely by the British going back to the colonial days, and had been the only bus company licensed to operate within the city with additional services to and from the suburbs, while a few private bus companies, which were Chinese-owned, were licensed to operate within the suburbs and rural areas, and very limited services to and from the city. The main Chinese-owned bus companies were merged by order of the government and directed to operate services to and from the city, which quickly led to the demise of the STC, which was already tottering and could not survive in that too-competitive environment any longer. Meanwhile, pirate or unlicensed taxis in aged and aging cars which used to ply main roads into and out of the city had been forced, through very strict enforcement ordered from above by the Traffic Police and Registry of Vehicles, out of business.

The PM was most concerned that there should not be the same or even similar traffic gridlock on Singapore's streets as he had observed in other cities on his official visits abroad, and ordered that the same should not happen in Singapore. I was of the view that a major problem vis-à-vis the apparent road traffic mess was the divided responsibility for road traffic, and commissioned the Management Services Department of MOF to undertake a study for possible solutions to that problem. The Management Services Department (MSD) recommended in its report that a statutory authority, the Road Transport Authority, be set up under Min Comm. My Minister and I were both in agreement. That was the conclusion we had drawn. We sent the report with our strong recommendation to the PM, whose blessing would be required to implement all or even some of the report's principal recommendations as it would involve changes to the portfolios of the relevant Ministers and their Ministries. But the Traffic Police, under the Home Affairs Ministry, and Roads Division of the Public Works Department, which came under the Ministry of National Development, were adamant that they would not hand over those responsibilities and the officers who went with them to Min Comm. The PM called a meeting of the Minister for Home Affairs, Minister for National Development and Minister for Communication, plus their Perm Secs and heads of the respective departments. The upshot of that meeting was the setting up of the Road Transport Action Committee (RTAC), under chairmanship of Perm Sec (Comm), me. The RTAC did get some improvements going but lacked the power and influence to really do enough. The RTAC was responsible for bringing in the Area Licensing Scheme (ALS) proposed by my good friend and classmate from St Andrew's School, the late Lim Leong Geok. Lim trained as an engineer in Adelaide, Australia, under the Colombo Plan and then headed the special unit under Min (Comm) set up to study such traffic problems, including a possible MRT which had yet to be approved. Lim Leong Geok had a big part to play behind the scenes for which he has not been given the recognition he should in planning and designing, and getting approved and going, the very first phase of Singapore's MRT. The ALS certainly did help road traffic in the city and it later evolved into the Area Road Pricing scheme. On the bus front, a Government Team of Officers (GTO) headed by another good personal friend of mine, Acting Perm Sec (Labour), Wong Hung Khim, and comprising several officers from the relevant government departments was sent into Singapore Bus Services Ltd (SBS), formed by the merger of all the remaining Chinese-owned private bus companies, to reorganise and operate SBS and its bus services. The GTO did very well in that difficult and most significant endeavour to stabilise and improve the bus services of Singapore.

Meanwhile a storm was brewing on our civil aviation front. Singapore had for long been delegated control, through the International Civil Aviation Organization (ICAO), over flights in the relevant Flight Information Region, mostly through Malaysian airspace, which was very much larger compared to Singapore's. Mainly owing to Singapore being the principal aviation hub of and for the region. Malaysia decided it would mount a bid at the next ICAO Regional Conference in Honolulu, Hawai'i, to reclaim its right to control all flights through its own airspace. I was delegated, as Perm Sec (Comm), to lead our team comprising the Director of Civil Aviation, Cheong Pak Chow, and representatives from the Republic of Singapore Air Force, Telecommunication Authority of Singapore and SIA. Perm Sec (Foreign Affairs), George Edwin Bogaars, was appointed advisor to the delegation. He was so appointed mainly owing to his own and his Ministry's very useful international lobbying, well before that ICAO Regional Conference in Honolulu, through its high commissioners, ambassadors and various other representatives overseas. Bogaars himself was a most influential, helpful and useful personal lobbyist with the ICAO regional representation in Bangkok and elsewhere. Our delegation managed to get ICAO's support to maintain the status quo in the delegated control over the relevant Flight Information Region with only minimal variation.

But while all that was boiling, bubbling and troubling in the road transport and civil aviation cauldrons, more was cooking in our Marine Department's hot pot. Negotiations were held with representatives from Malaysia to try to get the boundary in the Strait of Johore between Singapore and Malaysia surveyed, then fixed by coordinates. The boundary had been described since British times as the centre line of the deep water channel in the Straits. But, owing to shifts in the deep channel as a result of erosion and reclamation, the deep water channel had itself shifted over time and would no doubt shift even more over time unless it was fixed by coordinates. It was thought timely then to get a proper hydrographic survey done so that the centre line of the deep water channel could be denoted by coordinates and the international boundary fixed once and for all. This required agreement between Singapore and Malaysia as to who was to do the survey and how. The negotiations for that went rather smoothly, owing no doubt largely to the apparent joint willingness to seek and find the most suitable and best solution acceptable to both sides and interested third parties. Captain Goh Choo Keng, the Director of Marine and concurrently Portmaster on the Singapore side, and his team kept up a boisterous and most effective seafarers' camaraderie throughout the proceedings, lubricated most evenings by liberal doses of whisky at the Keppel Club in Singapore, near to Min (Comm) HQ and PSA HQ too. Captain Saito, the leader of the Japanese team assisting with the survey of the Malacca Sraits and a great friend of Captain Goh, was also a key player and champion truce-maker throughout the process of getting the Traffic Separation Scheme in the Malacca Straits going.

The decision to move the civil airport at Paya Lebar to Changi was what led to my being posted from Min Comm to the Education Ministry in 1976. Earlier, the plan had been to expand and grow Paya Lebar airport, where it was, to its full limit. International consultants had been commissioned under a United Nations Development Programme and had submitted plans for the projected expansion and growth of Paya Lebar. Construction there was already well underway, including the redirecting of a large stream that ran through the grounds over the former bed of which the new runway would be built. But the PM called my Minister one morning and asked that the expansion and growth plans for Paya Lebar be put aside while a new airport at Changi, which had been independently mooted by then PSA chairman Howe Yoon Chong, but not followed up on, be built instead. The PM stressed that Changi had a large tract of land suitable for a major civil airport, plus a seafront that was already partially reclaimed and that could be further reclaimed. In addition, the potential unknown danger from a runway built over the reclaimed bed of the stream at Paya Lebar would not be an issue at Changi. My Minister adamantly insisted that we should proceed with the planned and approved expansion of Paya Lebar, partly because so many resources had already been put to that use, as per the accepted recommendation of the specially appointed consultant. He expressed the view quietly to me that he believed the PM was peeved. On the eve of the PM's call, the PM had been harassed by several low-flying planes taking off or landing at Paya Lebar as he was officiating a function at a school in Tanjong Rhu nearby directly under the flight path of those planes. It turned out that while the PM had indeed been harassed by those planes, he was more concerned with the intrinsic benefit to Singapore of a brand new civil airport at Changi. The PM doggedly persisted and a new airport was built at Changi. It has gone on to expand several times since it first became operational in 1981, which would have been impossible at Paya Lebar. The move to Changi was undoubtedly a good decision.

The decision to move to Changi was correct and taken at the right time, when Singapore had the opportunity, capacity and means to embark on such a monumental and visionary task. But a lesson to be learnt from that whole episode, which applies equally to Singapore's maritime troubles and tribulations of the time, is that while Singapore needs to do what is best for Singapore, it also needs to consider its regional neighbours. For instance, with proper consultation, understanding and agreement, the Kuala Lumpur International Airport (KLIA) might well have been more fortuitously located north of Kuala Lumpur rather than south, at Subang, thus allowing KLIA to develop into an international air hub serving not only KL and central Peninsula Malaya but also the region north of KL and of Penang, Kota Bharu and environs, as well as southern Thailand and even very possibly across the Malacca

Straits to the central, eastern and northern provinces of Sumatra around Medan. Singapore's Changi might well then have also served the region of Peninsular Malaysia, south of KL and across the Malacca Straits to Riau, and the adjacent region of Sumatra.

The former Minister of the Ministry of National Development (MND) then became Minister for Communication and he asked for his former Perm Sec (MND), Sim Kee Boon, to accompany him there. And I, just before going on my December holiday to Jakarta, Yogyakarta and Bali, with my wife, Peggy, daughter, Karen, and son, Erwin Wei-Sung, was summoned to the office of the chairman, Public Service Commission (PSC), who told me I would have to move on. I would be going to the Ministry of Education (MOE), he declared, in the new year 1976, following my return from leave and visit to Indonesia with my family. When I demurred, not because I did not wish to be posted out of Min Comm but because I did not think I was up to the MOE job, saying I did not really believe I would be suitable for that job or be able to do it, the chairman told me not to worry. He said he had personally specially selected me for that job and had full confidence in me and my ability to do it. Besides, he was also sending a team, specially selected by him, comprising Dr Han Cheng Fong, Lim Hsiu Mei and N K Hazra, along with me to assist me and help me find the way in MOE, which came to be referred to at the time as "The Mystery of Education", and, he proclaimed, I should get on with that important task post haste. He added that in my new job I should first try to ascertain from school principals and teachers what their real problems were, rather than just presuming that HQ knew best in what was, to him, a very much top-down Ministry. The PM too himself asked for me to see him in his office where he also informed me of my imminent posting to the Ministry of Education in the new year, following my vacation with my family to Indonesia. So off I was once again to a new position, to try to understand and resolve that Mystery of Education. Ever the itinerant administrator, and like the proverbial rolling stone, unfortunately gathering no moss.

XII
Ministry of Education

The Ministry of Education (MOE) did not then have any resident full-time nor even part-time minister. The Minister for Home Affairs, who had his office at Phoenix Park, a short way along Tanglin Road to Kay Siang Road where the MOE was located, by special arrangement of the PM himself, also covered MOE. The PM himself was in effect unofficially in overall charge of MOE. Though, of course, the PM was responsible for the whole Cabinet and entire government machinery. Possibly owing to MOE being referred to on Radio Karat as the "Ministers' Graveyard", the Minister for Home Affairs went to the MOE HQ at Kay Siang Road only to chair a monthly meeting with the Permanent Secretary and his team of Admin Officers, the "Gang of Four", and the senior professional Education Service HQ officers. The draft minutes of those meetings were sent over to him at Phoenix Park for approval. The approved minutes were then circulated to those in attendance at the monthly meetings – just before the next ministerial meeting – for confirmation at the latter. This process took almost a month, thus leading to the Radio Karat commentary that the minutes were really just for the historical records in the National Archives and not for any real follow-up action. The Minister concentrated on his real portfolio at Home Affairs. There were a couple of Parl Secs, however, holed up at Kay Siang Road who did serve as some sort of liaison between the Minister, sitting at Phoenix Park, and MOE on occasion. That peculiar set up was indeed unique and quite a new experience for me.

I decided, to help me settle in and adapt to the MOE as early as I could, to take the advice of the PSC Chairman, which I thought was very good, to try to find out from the ground itself how the schools, and the MOE too, worked in practice and in relation to each other. So weekly school visits came to be instituted that were planned, organised and implemented by MOE's professional education officers' Research & Review Division, headed by professional education officer Lim Jit Poh. The Division produced occasional papers on topics, mainly arising out of the school visits, as well as on other topics of interest that were not deeply researched nor erudite dissertations, but rather useful guides to what possibly ailed our schools and the MOE's system or systems. A set of these papers, which I had collected over the duration of those school visits, was later presented by me, after I retired from the service, to the main library of the National University of Singapore (NUS) as an interesting historical record for the Faculty of Education at NUS, which evolved into the National Institute of Education at Nanyang Technological University. The name of the latter university reflects the wisdom and savvy of PM Lee Kuan Yew. When told the new name for the old Nanyang University would be Nanyang University of Technology, he said "No!" Because, he sagely observed, it would be abbreviated to NUT and its students and graduates and even lecturers and professors would most certainly be referred to as, "NUTs".

It was a difficult time for me and my team of three others at MOE, the Gang of Four. With no proper full-time minister, the PM became, effectively, minister-in-charge, which did not make it any easier but often more difficult as the PM had so many important and often urgent things to attend to and work on in office at the Istana some distance away. The PM often spoke to me on the phone for what were supposed to be dialogues, but turned out more often than not to be more akin to monologues. On one call he spoke for a continuous near hour, at the end of which he said, "Send me a note of our discussion." Discussion? I scratched my head. Throughout that near one-hour monologue I had taken no notes. I sat there staring blankly at the desk before me, then pulled out some blank sheets of paper and began to write. And wrote and wrote and wrote … till I had recorded all that I could recall and could recall no more of what the PM had said in that near one-hour phone call. I then got it typed out, as a draft, and sent it over to the PM's office. The PM apparently accepted the draft in full. It became then the official record of the PM's near one-hour monologue. On another occasion the PM directed me, in another phone monologue to get something done about the schools real quick. I told him it would take a good few months to fully implement, in a proper fashion. He asked, "Why?" I recounted the old Boy Scouts' tale of how a message whispered from ear to ear along the line became quite distorted and, more often than not, much different at the end of the line from what it was at the start. To avoid such mishap, which could be disastrous, I added that, with so many hundreds of schools and thousands of teachers, we had best first personally brief the MOE's professional officers, including the school inspectors, and the school principals in a single session at some sufficiently large school hall. Then the MOE professional officers, school inspectors and principals could themselves personally brief, in representative and manageable groups, the schoolteachers with record of each session to be checked and confirmed at each round to ensure no mistake or mishap. All this would take time and could not be rushed, lest a garbled version of what was intended was implemented. The PM did not say more, so I presumed he agreed. I took what time I thought we really needed to get it implemented. Such was my life then in MOE.

By the end of my first few years at MOE, I was convinced I had made little real headway in regard to what really mattered, and that I was unlikely to achieve anything more substantive if I stayed much longer. So I called on the PSC Chairman and told him I wanted out and why. He did not say more, but only told me to hold on and not do anything rash in the meantime. I knew he would have to consult the PM and needed time for that. As I surmised, I was soon called to the PM's office for a one-to-one chat. But I left that one-to-one chat with the PM hardly any wiser than before. Not too long after the Principal Private Secretary to the PM called me to say that a team led by the DPM, Dr Goh Keng Swee, would be going to MOE to undertake a review and make recommendations as to what might be needed in and for the MOE and Singapore's entire education and school system. I merely asked if the nominal Minister for Education knew or had been told about that and left it at that. Not too long after the nominal Minister for Education himself called me to say that Dr Goh and his team would make a study of and in the MOE.

I was invited to appear, once only, before Dr Goh and his team of system engineers to give my testimony. They all looked so disinterested to me in regard to what I might have to say that I was convinced it was only for form's sake to place on record that I had been consulted and invited to speak to them. Not too long after, I was once again to embark on yet another special assignment. This time to the Monetary Authority of Singapore (MAS). I volunteered to go as deputy managing director, rather than as second managing director (MD), so as not to unduly upset the serving MD, which would have doubtless made my one-year secondment there that much more difficult and uncomfortable.

Lim Jit Poh, who was by then Director, Vocational & Industrial Training Board (VITB), got his team from the Research & Review Division of the MOE to organise a farewell dinner for me, to which senior MOE HQ officers, school principals and even senior teachers were invited to participate should they so desire on a self-pay basis. My wife, Peggy, was invited too, to accompany me. It was a sell-out. The Shangri-La Hotel, with reputedly the largest ballroom in Singapore able to accommodate seventy circular dining tables, seating ten each, was filled to capacity. I was very much touched, and so was Peggy, by that show of regard and even affection from those MOE professional officers and school principals, and the few teachers too, who attended the dinner. A very senior secondary school principal, Neela Visvalingam who was my and Peggy's contemporary at the University of Malaya at Bukit Timah, gave a farewell speech in which she referred to the weekly school visits which, she declared, deeply affected school principals like her, who experienced for the very first time in their many years' service as teachers and school principals, an MOE Perm Sec visiting the schools, with a team of senior MOE HQ officers in tow, to meet and talk to school principals and their teachers to try to learn and understand their problems, rather than just summoning the principals to MOE HQ to order the school principals to do MOE HQ's bidding. It made me feel good and thankful to the PSC Chairman for his good advice to get to know the school principals and teachers in person and learn from them of their problems and, even more important, to tap them for any good ideas and suggestions.

Another very senior professional education officer at the MOE HQ, who also had been my contemporary at the University of

Malaya at Bukit Timah, Eugene Wijeysinghe, spoke as well. He recounted how I had, in my time at the MOE HQ, seemed to him like a Sphinx. All-seeing. All-hearing. All-knowing. But keeping mum. And doing nothing. In an off-the-cuff response, since I had not gone to the dinner in expectation of giving any speech, I remarked on how I had heard that the Sphinx had been eroding over the passage of time. So too, I said, had their very own MOE Sphinx. Hence I had to move on, to fresh fields and pastures new. Newspaper reporters and photographers at the dinner splashed stories and photos of the dinner and carried reports of the speeches in full in their newspapers the next day. It took me a long while to live all that down, amongst my fellow Perm Secs and non-MOE good friends.

XIII

Monetary Authority of Singapore, Ministry of Finance: Final Homecoming, Ministry of Law & Retirement

Life in the Monetary Authority of Singapore (MAS) was even more hectic and difficult for me. I had no briefing as to what my special assignment on secondment to MAS for an initial one year from 1980 was really for, nor what was expected of me. Except I did know that building up the management was of prime priority. I had to feel my way around and try to guess as best I could, which, of course, led often to my treading with heavy boots on many toes. I had asked, on being seconded to the MAS, for a team to be seconded too, to assist me in whatever I might be expected to do on that special assignment to the MAS, somewhat as had been done by the Public Service Commission Chairman himself, by way of the Gang of

Four, on my earlier special assignment to MOE in 1976. But that request was rejected. I was told, in no uncertain terms, I would be on my own. My special assignment to the MAS included the recruitment of the personnel needed for the MAS to become what it was expected it should be so it was up to me to recruit any team I might need myself. But whatever it was MAS was expected it to be, I had no idea. I had not actually been briefed on nor even vaguely told, but had to just guess and feel my way through whatever that way might be.

A computerisation consultant from the US, recruited earlier directly by the MAS, held a press conference in which he announced what would result from a joint computerisation plan for the MAS and the Board of Commissioners of Currency. The press conference, which got into the news and became very public, caused quite an uproar amongst certain ministers because that plan would not be in accord with the prevailing in-principle policy decision for the two bodies to remain separate and distinct. Almost immediately it was announced that DPM Goh Keng Swee was to move to the MAS and set things straight. This announcement led to the wags amongst my friends and colleagues in the ranks of the old time Perm Secs to proclaim that I was "a go getter because wherever you go, you get Goh!"

Before really getting into the thick of making changes at the MAS, Dr Goh commissioned a study by the Management Services Division (MSD) of the MOF, which reported, amongst other things, that the MAS was overstaffed and recommended that the excess staff be got rid of as expeditiously as possible. That task fell on me as head of admin in the MAS. Dr Goh had then to go on an official trip that he had earlier asked me to help arrange for him to a few selected leading banks and other financial institutions in Frankfurt, London, New York and San Francisco to learn from them how they did things and any good advice they might have to offer. He left me to be responsible for implementing the MSD's recommendations in his absence. I was therefore left with that unpleasant task and had no way to consult him nor seek his advice or help on what I should actually do or how best to do it in his absence. I therefore convened a meeting, which I alone chaired, in the MAS auditorium of all those who had been declared to be MAS excess staff. Notice of termination of service was to be served to each of those assembled in that auditorium at that meeting itself. I had thought it best to do that, rather than in dribs and drabs over some time, which would lead to rumours and speculation as to who, if anyone, would be next, and when, which I was convinced would not be at all good for the MAS itself and for its overall staff morale. But my plan, when put into action, led to big stories in the local newspapers and even some overseas journals. Headlines like "Bloodbath at MAS" appeared in print.

Following Dr Goh's return from his overseas trip and my assisting in implementation of whatever recommendations in the MSD report that were accepted remained, I was persuaded to agree to a six-month extension of my initial one-year secondment to MAS, which was coming to an end. Perm Sec (Finance) (Budget), George Edwin Bogaars, who attended weekly MAS meetings, asked me if I would go to the Budget Division of MOF following the end of my extended secondment, to take over from him as Perm Sec (Finance) (Budget), on his retirement on attaining his compulsory retirement age of fifty-five in October of 1981. George told me he would speak personally to the Minister for Finance about it and assured that he would put in a good word, should I wish to take over. The Finance Minister, Hon Sui Sen, was known as an old-school, kindly, gentleman boss, so I immediately said "Yes!" And it was done. A month or so before George's retirement, I moved to the

MOF on completion of my own extended secondment to the MAS. This was to be my final homecoming to the MOF. I understudied George for a while pending his retirement, before taking over from him as Perm Sec (Finance) (Budget).

I did enjoy working in the Budget Division of the MOF then and especially those great sessions of the Treasury Coffee Club (TCC), following my return to MOF. Every work day morning those Budget Boys, and girls too, would gather at a set time, in the room specially set aside for the purpose for our daily dose of coffee, tea or whatever, as long as it wasn't alcoholic, brewed in-house from stocks maintained by the Honorary Organising Secretary of TCC, H P M Noordin then. The TCC had been founded by George himself. When he was on special assignment some years earlier to head the Special Branch as the very first non-police director, he introduced what he termed "Morning Prayers". During which senior officers of Special Branch would meet when they could in a specially assigned room for coffee, tea or whatever every morning within a set time interval, so as to have an opportunity to informally meet to chat and exchange notes on anything non-classified. George felt it was needed for such a compartmentalised organisation as the Special Branch, wherein officers might otherwise not even get to meet informally. It enabled them to get to know each other at least and, hopefully, some idea of what others might be doing and of the overall direction of the organisation. He later introduced his "Morning Prayers" concept and sessions with very good effect in the Ministry of Foreign Affairs when he was posted there as Perm Sec, following his stint as Perm Sec (MID). It worked just as well, if not better, when he introduced it to the MOF, or the "Treasury", where it was reincarnated as the "Treasury Coffee Club". George was a gifted natural-born leader. His lesser colleagues, wherever he went, seemed to follow him most willingly with due regard and respect for him as a person and not just for his position. He was a good boss to work for and with, as his lesser work colleagues were often wont to declare.

In the Budget Division, on my posting there in 1981 as Perm Sec (Finance) (Budget), nothing too much was happening then of any real great national significance nor interest to me as Perm Sec (Finance) (Budget) or as a person. But, just prior to attainment of the retirement age of fifty-five, old-timer K R Chandra, sought in-principle approval for re-employment following retirement to his job as Perm Sec (Law). I put it, on behalf of Budget Division of the MOF to the PSC for its approval, as required by law. The PSC, in conveying approval for K R Chandra to be re-employed as Perm Sec (Law), on contract, also declared that K R Chandra should not draw the full salary of a Perm Sec on re-employment on contract following his retirement, but should draw that salary minus the value of the pension he would enjoy on retirement. I lazily passed the advice of the PSC on to Min Law myself without first consulting or even informing, my Minister, Minister of Finance Hon Sui Sen, not wanting to bother him unnecessarily. However, K R Chandra declared to his Minister, Minister for Law Eddie Barker, that he had no more desire to be re-employed on contract following retirement on such terms, which upset the Law Minister who immediately referred it to the PM, pointing out that the PSC had no jurisdiction over salaries under the law but only over appointments, promotions and terminations or dismissals. Which indeed was so. Hon Sui Sen, of course, then came to know about it and was undoubtedly much upset. He did not directly rebuke me at all, but did note in the relevant file that it appeared he had to be his own Permanent Secretary. That really hurt! And caused me much heartache over having caused such a dastardly deed to so kind and gentlemanly a boss through my negligence. I grieved even more, when sometime later, Minister Hon Sui Sen passed away from a heart attack while in hospital. Especially as, a few days before that sad event, I had led a few senior Perm Secs on a visit to the Minister in hospital. Minister Hon Sui Sen's passing was a great loss to the nation and deeply upset me.

Before he retired, K R Chandra asked if I would be interested in taking over from him as Perm Sec (Law), concurrent with my appointment then as PS (Finance) (Budget). He told me he had spoken already to his long-time Minister, Eddie Barker, who most readily agreed but told Chandra he thought the PM possibly might not be agreeable. He had previously offered to take George Bogaars as his Perm Sec when George was about to be moved out of his appointment as Perm Sec elsewhere, but it was objected to on the grounds that it would not do for both the Minister and his Perm Sec to be of the same ethnic minority of Singapore: Eurasian. Nevertheless, when Minister for Law, Eddie Barker, did seek approval for me to take over from K R Chandra, it was approved without questions as I was later informed. It was interesting and pleasant to have Eddie Barker for a boss, as he was an appreciative Minister, always willing to listen and more akin to a respected senior colleague than crusty old boss. It was not too difficult either, doubling up as Perm Sec (Finance) (Budget) and Perm Sec (Law). I usually spent mornings at the CPF Building, where the MOF then was, and also at City Hall then Raffles City, in the afternoon, where Min Law was and later moved to. Come 1986, I was summarily told I would have to give up the post of Perm Sec (Finance) (Budget), so someone else could take over. I then became just Perm Sec (Law), minus Perm Sec (Finance) (Budget) and remained so until my retirement in 1989, aged almost fifty-six, the minimum age for optional retirement being fifty-five.

When I was to depart the MOF for the last time on moving from dual Perm Sec (Finance) (Budget)-cum-Perm Sec (Law) to the Ministry of Law (Min Law) as solely Perm Sec (Law), some of my Budget Boys led by kaypoh Ajith Prasad came to my office to commiserate with me for having to leave MOF and go down, in their estimation, from the prestigious dual role of Perm Sec (Finance) (Budget)-cum-Perm Sec (Law) to the lowly single appointment of Perm Sec (Law). I told them not to worry. For, I gently explained, it was in effect a promotion for me. They looked askance, pitying my apparent loss of sanity brought on, no doubt they surmised, by what must have been in expectation of that traumatic demotion their old big boss was about to suffer. So I very carefully explained that while I was in MOF holding that single appointment of Perm Sec (Finance) (Budget) and ordered to also be Perm Sec (Law) with no increase at all in salary, it was in effect a demotion for me. But when I was ordered to move on to Min Law as only Perm Sec (Law), with no loss in earnings, it would in effect be a big promotion for me. Ajith and his Budget Boys looked at me with some relief, no doubt partially assured their departing big boss had not totally lost all his marbles! No doubt in my heyday in Budget Division there must certainly have been occasions galore when Ajith and his Budget Boys thought that their big boss was completely insane! For instance, when I proclaimed that I hoped one day the Budget Division and my Budget Boys, Ajith included, could bring budgeting out from the depths of witchcraft to the higher realm of science.

Upon my departure from the MOF for the very last time those great Budget Boys and Girls, gave me a most memorable farewell dinner and send-off. The original Honorary Organising Secretary TCC, H P M Noordin, gave an impassioned farewell address in his usual impeccable style. He was the real star of that show. I had wanted to retire the previous year on attainment of my minimum optional age for retirement of fifty-five, but my then Minister, Eddie Barker, had dissuaded me, and urged me not to desert him. After he had retired himself as Minister for Law, I had no restraint and applied for optional retirement, although by then Minister for Home Affairs S Jayakumar had taken over the Minister for Law portfolio from Eddie Barker. Jayakumar had been a law student and freshie of mine at the University of Malay at Bukit Timah and I knew him well and found him a very good boss to work for. In support of my application was that if I retired at age fifty-five or -six, it would allow me ten years or so in the corporate sector. I added that, after so many eventful years of public service, including being there at the very birth of the Republic of Singapore, I would like if possible to experience life, for a few years at least, in a second career in the corporate sector before finally retiring from active working life. After my retirement from the public service, a few months short of the age of fifty-six, I moved into the corporate sector, though essentially in government-linked companies (GLCs).

In 1988, before my retirement from public service, the then Dean of the Faculty of Arts & Social Sciences of NUS, Professor Edwin Thumboo, Peggy's and my contemporary at the University of Malaya at Bukit Timah, and a good personal friend of mine from our undergrad days, invited me as the guest of honour, together with Peggy, to the NUS Faculty of Arts & Social Sciences annual dinner. Where and when I was also to deliver an annual address. I was told to keep to not more than twenty minutes and ensure it was neither too heavy nor too light, but interesting enough to hold the attention of such an august audience at an annual dinner. I recounted my experiences at the university, and the life of the university itself, from when it had morphed in 1949 into the University of Malaya from the former Raffles College and King Edward VII College of Medicine; became the University of Singapore; and finally the

National University of Singapore. I added I could possibly, in theory, have been a graduate of the old University of Malaya at Bukit Timah, then a postgraduate of the University of Singapore and finally a postgraduate PhD of the National University of Singapore. In effect, a graduate of one and postgraduate of two, though in fact from the same university, but under different names. I also recounted how Peggy, who had a postgraduate master's in library science from the University of Chicago, had been pursued by the latter to maintain that connection and make donations if and when able to the University of Chicago from the time of her return to Singapore from Chicago till the present. I suggested NUS would do well to follow suit and do as much if not more to preserve and keep going for as long as possible enduring links to its alumni. I am most happy to note that the NUS Development Office was later established specifically for that purpose, though I do not claim nor could I that my address that night at the NUS Faculty of Arts & Social Sciences Annual Dinner was what caused the NUS Development Office to come into being.

On learning of my impending retirement from the civil service, then Perm Sec (Foreign Affairs) Peter Chan told me, when I happened to meet him at an official dinner, that a couple of his senior foreign service officers, who had served as ambassadors themselves and one of whom had worked as a new young officer with me at MID, had prevailed upon him to get me appointed as a high commissioner or ambassador. He said, if I agreed, he would take the necessary action to get it done. I explained to Peter Chan that a great part of my wishing to retire from civil service was to allow me the opportunity and time to be with my wife, Peggy, when needed. She had had surgery in 1983, followed by chemo and radiotherapy, after which her cancer was in remission. However, the cancer had begun to flare up again and the prognosis then was none too optimistic. Being a full-time high commissioner or ambassador would not allow me the opportunity nor time to be with her when she most needed me. I added, however, that I would be prepared to consider serving as non-resident high commissioner or ambassador. Peter told me he understood and would pursue the idea of appointing me non-resident high commissioner or ambassador, which he most promptly did.

XIV

Afterlife 1: Non-Resident High Commissioner

My retirement from the civil service took effect from February 1989 – a couple of months before my fifty-sixth birthday. My first appointment as non-resident high commissioner was to Mauritius in 1990. The city, with its government offices and commercial centre, was at Port Louis while the presidential palace, where the president resided and operated from, was some way inland up a mountainside. Presentation of my credentials as High Commissioner for the Republic of Singapore took place at the presidential palace. Sometime later, at a garden party in the grounds of the presidential palace to celebrate Independence Day, I was in an interesting conversation with a genial old Indian Mauritian gentleman. As we walked steadily towards the edge of the vast garden that overlooked a forested valley and the open sky beyond, I noticed a beautiful rainbow arching over the valley, through dense mist rising up from the valley. I quietly, in all seriousness, remarked on what a beautiful and wonderful rainbow it was and signified how lucky that Independence Day must be for the people of Mauritius, for such a beautiful and wonderful rainbow was surely a good omen. The gentleman kept silent for a while but glanced at the rainbow then looked hard at me a couple of times, before quietly saying, "But, you know, we do get that rainbow here most evenings, around this time. It happens when the mist thrown up by the waterfall cascades and the setting sun shines through." I did not know what to say nor where to hide my face. My comment had been well intended but obviously turned out to be such a boo-boo! I was saved from more such embarrassment by a waiter with a tray loaded with drinks and titbits who came walking by. I ordered a drink refill from that waiter for the kindly Mauritian gentleman, gratefully grabbed a strong one for myself, and proposed a toast to Mauritius and its peoples.

Mauritius I found to be a most interesting place with its mix of largely Indian Mauritians; some of European descent, mainly French and English; and a sprinkling of those of Chinese descent. I was told by one of those of Chinese descent – Hakka he said proudly – a most interesting story. The Chinese, both Cantonese and Hakka, had been brought to Mauritius to work as indentured labourers on cane plantations. But the Cantonese and Hakka soon ganged up against each other. The Cantonese lost and were driven out of Mauritius and took refuge in the neighbouring French territorial Reunion Isles. Mauritius was colonised initially by the French who later were replaced by the British, on condition that the French language, culture and customs were allowed to continue and flourish side by side with those of the English. It was interesting to hear native-born adult Mauritians of both Chinese and Indian descent speak English and also their French-Creole. I met a Mauritian Chinese dental surgeon and his wife who was Cantonese and from Hong Kong she proudly declared. She was quite surprised and happy too to hear me speak to her in her

Cantonese dialect with whatever words I knew and could recall. Though she did remark, very good naturedly, that my intonation was terrible. She, and her husband too, had a good laugh when I explained that my wife was Cantonese and that in our early days of marriage, when our daughter Karen was still a toddler, I had asked our old-fashioned black-and-white Cantonese amah, passed on to my wife Peggy by her mother, for my slippers in Cantonese on getting home from work. Peggy very promptly ordered me to never again speak in Cantonese at home, lest I corrupt our little daughter Karen, because my tones were so awful, and my intonation made some words I spoke, or attempted to, sound vulgar and very coarse, or, at least, like words that should not be used in the presence of a young innocent child. The Mauritian Chinese dental surgeon and his wife from Hong Kong had a good laugh. We became very good friends following that, and would meet, whenever we could, for an informal and relaxing dinner with good French wine abundantly available and served on my visits to Mauritius thereafter.

Not too long after I was concurrently appointed High Commissioner for the Republic of Singapore to Tanzania. It was a large, rambling country, especially compared to Mauritius, with many very interesting places to visit. In particular the famed Mount Kilimanjaro, which I did get the opportunity to visit, though not to the top. I also visited Zanzibar and the sultan's palace there, to which I made an official call; and to the one-time capital-to-be, Dodoma, where a sitting of parliament was then on; and also to the Serengeti; and into the huge extinct volcano crater of Ngorongoro; and, of course, to Dar-es-Salaam, the capital, where I usually stayed and presented my credentials as high commissioner and made my official calls on my visits. Tanzania was a place for safaris of various kinds and interesting as well, including its peoples. On one visit to Dar-es-Salaam we happened to meet a Chinese man relaxing by the poolside of the hotel I usually stayed at on my visits. We got talking in a smattering of English and Mandarin, which my aide from MFA was fluent in, and discovered our new friend from China and his wife had been in Dar-es-Salaam for quite a while and had an ongoing traditional Chinese medicine clinic there where they offered reflexology, tuina and some traditional medications. There was a thriving Chinese community there they said from the People's Republic of China, right from the time of the initiation of the China-built railway. They invited us to their small home one night, for a home-cooked Chinese meal.

I was next asked, in 1992, to also cover South Africa, following Nelson Mandela's release from his long incarceration and when apartheid was on its way out, and the general election for the very first multi-ethnic or "Rainbow Nation" Parliament – as Mandla was wont to say – was on the way in. I was to help pave the way for a visit to South Africa later in 1992 of then Senior Minister Lee Kuan Yew. He had been invited by a prominent English-language newspaper there, as the keynote speaker for a big conference that newspaper was sponsoring. Since Singapore had not yet established diplomatic relations with the Republic of South Africa and had made it clear that it would not till after the general election of 1994 to a multi-ethnic parliament and installation of a new president, expected to be Nelson Mandela of the once-banned African National Congress (ANC), it was agreed I should initially be Special Representative of Singapore to South Africa with diplomatic immunity and status no less than that of any accredited diplomatic representative to South Africa of any other country, which I had insisted on as being prerequisite for the work expected of me as the Special Representative of Singapore to South Africa.

On my first visit to South Africa as Special Representative for Singapore I was treated right royally in no small measure owing to groundwork laid down in advance of my visit by the late William Hung, a well-connected ethnic Chinese South African businessman who had been introduced to me by my very good friend the late Charlie Phua, senior marketing executive of the then Singapore state trading corporation Intraco Ltd. On my first official call on the Foreign Minister in his office at Pretoria, the Minister most kindly offered to arrange a complimentary special helicopter ride over Capetown for me accompanied by William Hung, which I had planned to do in any case, and made good on his offer by arranging an excellent helicopter ride over Capetown for me accompanied by William Hung.

While in Johannesburg I made a special call, accompanied by William Hung who diligently accompanied me on most of my other calls during that visit, on ANC HQ in Shell Tower. Walking together from our hotel along streets we had been warned would not be safe. We went to seek support and welcome from ANC for the call on Nelson Mandela planned for Senior Minister Lee Kuan Yew in the course of his visit to South Africa for the newspaper conference at which he was to deliver the keynote address. I also called on principal officers of the newspaper at whose conference Senior Minister Lee Kuan Yew was to deliver the keynote address, and on those at the hotel too where the conference would be held and at which Senior Minister Lee Kuan Yew, Mrs Lee and members of the delegation were to stay during the conference. We took advantage of that call to also check out the hotel itself and its facilities. It was a very busy but most fruitful and interesting visit to and in Johannesburg with William Hung keeping me good company much of the time and dispensing good advice along the way.

Later that year I accompanied Senior Minister Lee Kuan Yew and Mrs Lee plus delegation to the big conference in Johannesburg hosted by that newspaper. When they left after the conference to go on a visit to a nature reserve, I returned to Singapore for a few days just to chair the annual general meeting of Neptune Orient Lines (NOL) of which I was then non-executive chairman. Following that I immediately flew to Mauritius to receive Senior Minister Lee Kuan Yew, Mrs Lee and party on arrival for their official visit to Mauritius. That visit to Mauritius went extremely well with Senior Minister Lee Kuan Yew, Mrs Lee and delegation welcomed with much warmth. I was to make my final diplomatic visit as High Commissioner for the Republic of Singapore to Mauritius soon after. In accord with my agreement with MFA that I should relinquish that appointment on assuming appointment as High Commissioner for the Republic of Singapore to the Republic of South Africa following the general election there in 1994 and election and installation of Nelson Mandela as the first ANC President of the Republic of South Africa. In accord with that agreement I was also to be accredited as Non-Resident High Commissioner to Botswana, Namibia and Swaziland in addition to the Republic of South Africa.

Not too long after the installation of President Mandela, which I attended as co-representative of the Republic of Singapore with Finance Minister Dr Richard Hu, I presented my credentials as the very first High Commissioner of the Republic of Singapore to the Republic of South Africa of the freshly elected and installed President Nelson Mandela of the African National Congress (ANC) at Stadthuys in Capetown. It was a simple ceremony in a historic setting of most pleasant Capetown at which envoys of a few other countries also presented credentials in turn. There was then, we were told, a backlog of envoys from various countries awaiting their turn to present credentials.

As I had also, perhaps most foolishly looking back, agreed with the then Singapore Foreign Minister to take on, concurrently with non-resident appointment to South Africa, appointments as Non-Resident High Commissioner to Botswana, Namibia and Swaziland, soon I was calling at Gaborone in Botswana, at Windhoek in Namibia and at Mbabane in Swaziland to present my credentials as the very first ever High Commissioner for the Republic of Singapore. Not long after, I made a visit to South Africa, Botswana and Namibia with a team from our Ministry of Foreign Affairs, led by a senior officer from MFA HQ, T Jasudasen, on a visit to those countries to pave the way for an official visit to the countries by PM Goh Chok Tong not long after. He was to visit with a delegation of senior officials from MFA including T Jasudasen and others from various ministries and departments, plus representative businessmen who had been specially invited to join. The visit was to be made in a private Boeing 747, owned by the Sultan of Brunei who had kindly offered to loan it to Singapore for that visit in response to a personal request by Senior Minister Lee Kuan Yew. That Boeing 747 came with a fully operational cockpit and cabin crew, at no cost, at the insistence of the Sultan, to the government of Singapore, except for the cost of fuel and airport and ground charges at the airports in the respective countries we visited, which Lee Kuan Yew insisted in turn Singapore should pay for. Thus we saved, not only the cost of aircraft and crew that would have otherwise have to be specially chartered, but also the hassle of seeking and obtaining approvals, permits and the like, especially in countries where such things could be quite difficult to organise as I had learnt only too well when I was Administrative Secretary for the delegation led by then DPM Dr Toh Chin Chye and Foreign Minister S Rajaratnam to the UN in New York and beyond in 1965.

Prior to that official visit by PM Goh Chok Tong to South Africa, Botswana and Namibia, I made a visit as part of a small delegation from our Ministry of Foreign Affairs to the three countries to prime them on the intended official visits and what was sought for and from them, as well as to try and get as much of the hoped-for programmes tentatively arranged as possible. Following that, I made visits to the three countries myself, in my capacity as high commissioner, in advance of the PM's official visits, to check on and reconfirm or confirm plans, arrangements and programmes. The official visits by PM Goh Chok Tong and delegation, in that very comfortably fitted out private Boeing 747, to South Africa, Botswana and Namibia went off exceedingly well. They were most interesting and pleasant visits, with PM Goh Chok Tong and delegation being received very well indeed.

On first being appointed non-resident High Commissioner to South Africa, Botswana, Namibia and Swaziland, I had planned to make two diplomatic visits per year to South Africa, plus at least one, if not two, to the other countries of my accreditation. In the event I did manage to largely keep to that schedule but found it far more difficult and tiring as time went on. Moreover, although it had initially been agreed that non-resident ambassadors or NRAs would travel first class while on their representational duties, MFA Admin suddenly unilaterally declared that NRAs would henceforth have to be downgraded from first class. I decided then it would best for me to give up my appointments as Non-Resident High Commissioner to South Africa, Botswana, Namibia and Swaziland as the travel might be too much of a strain. And promptly did so. However, after I gave up all those appointments I was called on by the Ministry of Foreign Affairs, from time to time as the need arose, to go on special missions to some, if not all, of those countries, plus others, as Special Representative of the Ministry of Foreign Affairs. Those were purpose-specific and rather brief and compressed visits but quite interesting, on which I often had the opportunity to meet old friends from my earlier life as non-resident high commissioner.

XV

Afterlife 2: Singapore Turf Club

On my last diplomatic visit to Mauritius, when I returned to my hotel following a couple of appointments, I found a telex – yes, we were still using telexes then – awaiting me in my room. It was from Dr Goh Keng Swee, then Chairman of the Singapore Totalisator Board, which had overall responsibility of the then Bukit Turf Club. The earlier Singapore Turf Club, a private members' club, had been acquired lock, stock and barrel by the government for fear that it might be in imminent danger of being dissolved by its newly elected management committee chaired by a non-Singaporean, and all assets of the club including cash reserves of tens of millions of Singapore dollars and extensive holding of prime land would be consequently distributed in specie to its privileged few members. Following the government's acquisition of the club, my former Minister in Min Law Eddie Barker, a keen horse racing fan himself and former racehorse owner, had been installed by the government as chairman of the club, which was renamed Bukit Turf Club, along with a freshly appointed management committee. In his telex to me, Dr Goh stated he was informed I had agreed with the PM to take over chairmanship of the club after Eddie Barker who had relinquished the post. Hence, Dr Goh added, I should see him in his office at the Totalisator Board upon my return from Mauritius to discuss and settle arrangements for my taking over, as well as plans for the club thereafter. I telexed in response that I had no recollection of any such agreement on my part with the PM. Nevertheless, I would be happy to meet Dr Goh in his office on my return. Which I very promptly did.

And so it came to pass I was Chairman of the Bukit Turf Club. Following which, not too long after, the management committee and only-too-eager management of the club reverted the club name to the Singapore Turf Club as soon as it legally and most conveniently could be done. A principal task for us was to plan, get going and done the government-ordered move of the entire club, including the racetrack, stables and everything that went with thoroughbred horse racing, to the still-to-be-developed government-designated site, on which stood a large septic tank that served the locality and was capped, on insistence of former Chairman Eddie Barker, to avoid any stink. The new site was located next to the Kranji War Memorial and not yet served by any road network. The new clubhouse, racetrack, stables and all the facilities for thoroughbred horse racing were to be paid for entirely by the government, in compensation for acquisition of the cash reserves and very sizeable valuable land at Bukit Timah. Under its previous regime, revenue garnered by the Singapore Turf Club in excess of expenditure requirements was to be donated to charity. But in reality the old turf club had been niggardly in donating to charity and had built up a sizeable nest egg of reserve funds from its revenue excess. Following the acquisition, all revenue earned was instead to go to the Totalisator Board which, in turn, would allocate a budget each year to the club based on its board-approved expenditure budget. Making the club, in effect, a beggar for its own hard-earned revenue.

Planning, organising and getting a move on and done for the fresh site at Kranji, within less than five years from 1994 to 1999, was in itself a monumental task. Meanwhile the club had to continue horse racing at the old site at Bukit Timah, which had been operational since 1933, on rotation with its three sister clubs in Malaysia – Selangor Turf Club at Kuala Lumpur, Perak Turf Club at Ipoh and Penang Turf on the island of Penang itself – under the overall auspices of the venerable Malayan Racing Association (MRA). Regular meetings were held by the MRA committee to oversee racing on rotation in Peninsula Malaysia and in Singapore. Those committee meetings were held in turn at each of the three clubs in Malaysia and at the Singapore Turf Club to coincide with the race dates of the respective clubs. However, this arrangement and the consequent movement of horses between Singapore and Malaysia came to an abrupt end with the outbreak of the nipah virus in Malaysia. Singapore continued to race under the overall MRA umbrella but without rotation of racing with the sister clubs in Malaysia nor any movement of racehorses to and from Malaysia, which strained the club's resources and facilities, still based at Bukit Timah, and threw up a whole host of thorny new problems for the management committee and management to resolve or shelve. Luckily, and owing to the hard work put in by the management committee and management, the new racecourse and related amenities and facilities at Kranji were ready for occupation and regular racing by 1999, and within the approved budget. This was an achievement in itself, for which the management committee and management of the Singapore Turf Club should be and were justifiably proud.

Regular racing at Kranji began in 1999. There were trial runs prior to the unofficial opening day for regular racing. But on the unofficial opening day itself, our usual guests from our three sister race clubs in Malaysia and the club's regular public patronage, were dismayed when the floodlights necessary for night racing suddenly went out. Neither the Singapore Turf Club nor any of its sister clubs in Peninsula Malaysian had ever had the lighting facilities for night racing before. It was a novelty in the MRA for which the Singapore Turf club had to fight hard in MRA committee meetings, in order for night racing to be introduced only to Singapore while none of the turf clubs in Malaysia were able to do so. But on that day of the soft opening, the racetrack and its surrounds at Kranji plunged into darkness. It took quite a while for the lights to be fixed. Meanwhile, there was scrambling here, there and everywhere of supervisors, technicians and workmen, each seeking how best to try to set things right in the shortest time possible and save the reputation of the Singapore Turf Club and, of course, of the club's chairman too. They did manage to get it fixed in not too long a while. The racetrack floodlights came back on to loud cheers. Night racing thenceforth at Kranji became a regular feature of the Singapore Turf Club.

In the following year, 2000, came the grand official opening of the new clubhouse and racecourse at Kranji by President of the Republic of Singapore and Honorary Patron of the Singapore Turf Club, S R Nathan. The club also hosted the very first international race in Singapore and the entire MRA circuit: the Singapore Airlines International Race with record prize money of $3 million. The prize money was mostly contributed by the Singapore Turf Club itself, while Singapore Airlines, after which the international race was named was prepared to contribute not more than $200,000. That grand official opening of the Kranji racecourse in 2000 and the Singapore Airlines International Race were televised across the horse racing world, which responded most favourably. The race was run by highly rated racehorses from a good number of noted racing and breeding countries. It positioned Singapore very clearly on the world map of thoroughbred horse racing.

With the cessation of horse racing in Singapore on rotation with the other MRA clubs in Peninsula Malaysia, owing to the nipah virus, Singapore had to mount racing at Kranji far more frequently than before. This required new stables for the many more new horses to be stabled, trained and raced at Kranji. The consultant, who had been responsible for the planning, design and overseeing construction of the racecourse at Kranji was commissioned to come up with a workable proposal that could then be put to to the Totalisator Board that had, by order and design of the government, authority over the club's entire expense requirements, capital and recurrent. The consultant's cost estimate for the additional stables and related facilities on the vacant land between the racetrack at Kranji and the main road that ran towards Johore in southern Peninsula Malaysia was approximately $200 million, which, when put to him, must have shocked the then Chairman of the Totalisator Board who had taken over from the previous Chairman, Dr Goh. He reacted immediately by rejecting outright the proposed capital budget and to stem what he must have deemed profligacy of the Chairman of the Singapore Turf Club, the Chairman of the Totalisator Board appointed a special committee to forthwith most carefully scrutinise the club's entire budget expenditure proposals and make their findings and recommendations to the Totalisator Board. It wasn't too much earlier that the Totalisator Board had reluctantly agreed, after protracted toing-and-froing, to allocate only a very modest annual budget out of the earnings of the club to the club for donation to charity in the latter's name. Which, in fact, was what the earnings of the club were originally intended for. Hence the decisions of the Totalisator

Board in regard to the proposal for new additional stables and related facilities rankled all the more. I tendered my resignation as chairman, effective in 2001, some seven years into my appointment, following the second year of the Singapore Airlines International Race. I did everything I could to promote the standard of horse racing to a higher level and on a more permanent basis than it had been before and then I relinquished the appointment of Chairman of the Singapore Turf Club.

Before relinquishing appointment as Chairman of Singapore Turf Club, following the Singapore Airlines International Race I was invited to attend the internationally renowned races in Kentucky. I flew on Singapore Airlines (SIA) from Singapore to San Francisco for a change of flight there on to Kentucky. I was met at the airport in Kentucky by Soong, the club's racing manager. He gave me a peculiar smile, then said with a big wide grin while shaking my hand most vigorously, "Glad to see you!" He explained that he had been told I had been initially booked on the SIA flight out of Singapore with a transit at Taipei and onward from there to Los Angeles, to change flight there and on to Kentucky. But he had later been informed my SIA flight out of Singapore had been changed at my request to transit at Hong Kong and on from there to San Francisco instead. I confirmed that it was indeed so, as I much preferred the timing of the arrival in San Francisco and out from there to Kentucky. The racing manager then burst out, "You very lucky man!" He explained, looking at me almost like I was a ghost, that the SIA flight I had originally been booked on had crashed while on the tarmac at the airport in Taipei, killing some passengers and cabin crew. Later, we discovered the mother of a trainer at the Singapore Turf Club, who had gone on a visit to Singapore from the US, specially to attend the 2001 Singapore Airlines International Race at the invitation of her son, had unfortunately been killed in the crash.

XVI

Afterlife 3: Export Credit Insurance Corporation

When I was seconded on special assignment to the Monetary Authority of Singapore (MAS) in 1980, I was tasked to take over as non-executive chairman of the Export Credit Insurance Corporation of Singapore (ECICS). A company set up by the government, in which it was the principal shareholder, with various banks and other financial institutions in Singapore subscribing to the remainder. Its objective was to help promote the large-value export of goods and services from Singapore by providing insurance cover for the capital costs of such exports against default of payment therefor. It had then been in the doldrums. Export companies in Singapore did not find such insurance cover necessary or not sufficient when they did wish such insurance. They would seek to select against ECICS as to which exports to insure when they did seek to insure, rather than insure all. There was then a boom in oil rig newbuilding in Singapore, with the bulk of the oil rig newbuilds being exported to Nigeria and other such oil-producing countries, leading to too much exposure for ECICS to carry on its own. The co-sharing of such risks with the Ministry of Finance had also been brought to an abrupt end, by the Minister, owing to over-exposure. The then managing director of ECICS, on loan from the UK Export Guarantee Department and under UNDP sponsorship, looked to offer insurance for the business of confirming houses to make up for the loss of the oil rig export business. But that led to fresh problems and the consequent abrupt departure of that managing director. I decided then to engage a new managing director for ECICS, and after a search decided on Foo Kok Swee who was then CEO of Heller Factoring, an American-owned factoring company in Singapore. He had been in the Logistics Division of MID when I too was there as DMP, from 1965 to 1967, and I knew him personally.

Foo Kok Swee went about trying to set things right in ECICS as best he could. Among other things he persuaded me to go with him to Nigeria where the bulk of payments due on oil rigs exported from Singapore had been frozen by the Nigerian government. He had asked for assurance, and been assured before he accepted the job as the CEO of ECICS, he would not be held personally responsible for losses as a result of defaults prior to his appointment. Kok Swee as CEO agreed with me as chairman on one of those visits to Lagos to appoint as ECICS' collecting agent in Nigeria, Aremu Olashoju, a Nigerian businessman who had been introduced to us by the Indian Tata representative in Lagos, who in turn had been introduced to us by my good friend in our state-trading company Intraco Ltd, Gopinath Pillai, who was then also on the Board of ECICS. Over a relatively short span of time, ECICS, through the auspices of Olashoju, recovered the bulk of those frozen payments in Nigeria amounting to several hundred million Singapore dollars. Olashoju would personally meet Foo Kok Swee and I at the airport in Lagos whenever we arrived to take us to our hotel in his car.

His chauffeur would slow down at any checkpoint on the road, and Olashoju, who would be seated in the front passenger seat, would wind down the car window and stick out his hand to shake the hands of the armed guards, who would then wave us on with big smiles. Olashoju seemed to us to be very well known and much liked. He was a tribal Nigerian, with tribal scars across both his cheeks, who had converted to Christianity some time before to marry his wife, who was a staunch Christian. On Foo Kok Swee's and my calls on the Finance and Trade Ministries in Lagos, to chase up monies due to ECICS, Olashoju would also go with us there and back in his chauffeur-driven car. Again, when we arrived at the gates of those Ministries, which were always shut tight, to keep out the crowd that would invariably be milling around outside, Olashoju would make sure to stick out his hand to shake the hand or hands of the guard or guards who would then smilingly wave us through. Olashoju's chauffeur would park the car as near as he could to the entrance that led to the lift going straight up to the office of the Minister that we were to call on. The attendant for that lift, standing by, would immediately open the lift door and take Olashoju and us straight up to the designated floor. We found Olashoju to be a most effective agent for ECICS in Lagos.

Kok Swee and I also went to other countries to seek similar release of frozen credit payments. Principally to Indonesia, where bank interest on US dollar charges, which were much lower than the comparative interest rates for charges in Indonesian rupiah, turned drastically following the Indonesian authorities' abrupt freezing of all US dollar payments. A memorable visit we made was to Palu, Sulawesi, to check on some barges and bulldozers stuck out in some remote part of the island. We drove out to a small slipway someway outside Palu in a four-wheel drive utility on rough mud tracks to where a couple of barges were moored. We found both barges to be in what appeared to us as reasonable condition. But those barges were then not permitted to leave that mooring, so there was nothing we could do but take note and depart. As for the bulldozers, we were told that both had fallen into an unchartered ravine while trying to clear the way through the jungle for a mud track. It would cost much more to retrieve them than they were worth. So we decided to not even bother to go out into the jungle to check on them, or to determine if they were even really there, but to write them off and go back to Palu and from there to Jakarta, then back to Singapore. Mission completed, but nothing much really accomplished.

To make up for the loss of all such business to ECICS, Kok Swee proposed that ECICS buy out all its bank co-shareholders, and venture into new business, namely factoring. Foo Kok Swee himself had personal experience in his previous life as CEO of the American-owned Heller Factoring, so we proceeded as he recommended. ECICS founded stand-alone and wholly owned International Factors (Singapore) Ltd. To grow the factoring business, Kok Swee recommended setting up joint venture factoring companies with bank partners in Bangkok, Jakarta and Manila, which we did. This, of course, involved travelling to Bangkok, Jakarta and Manila to attend board meetings and the like of the joint venture factoring in those three countries.

Following one such meeting in Jakarta, Kok Swee and I were in the SIA lounge in Chengkareng Airport, waiting for our SIA flight to Singapore. The flight was to arrive in Jakarta from Singapore, then return. But its departure had been delayed and it had not by then left Singapore when the SIA station manager came up to Kok Swee and me in the lounge to offer to put us both on a Silk Air flight to Singapore, which was about to depart. But he warned that there was no first class on that flight and, while he could put us both in two of the few seats still available, we had to accept whatever was available and could not preselect seats. Kok Swee was keen to accept that offer. He explained that he had a dinner appointment that night in Singapore and, if we waited for the delayed flight, he might well get into Singapore very late for his dinner appointment or even too late to attend. I told Kok Swee to go ahead if he wished, but I would rather sit and wait in the comfortable lounge at Chengkareng with plenty to eat and drink, and newspapers and magazines to read, as well as television to watch. Besides, I told him, the ride back to Singapore on that Silk Air flight would be far less comfortable than in the original first class on Singapore Airlines. Kok Swee changed his mind and elected to wait with me at Chengkareng for the delayed flight, which got into Chengkareng just over an hour late. By the time we got into Singapore, our SIA flight was more than two hours past the original estimated time of arrival. We both got into our separate waiting cars, with drivers, and made our way home. The next morning, we got news of the loss of that Silk Air flight into a river estuary in Sumatra. No survivors were reported from amongst passengers or crew.

International Factors (Singapore), IFS, continued to grow under the auspices of ECICS and the diligent perseverance of its two senior executives, Kwah Thiam Hock and Nagantha (John) Pillay, who had faithfully seen ECICS through its most difficult days. IFS was rather successfully listed on the Stock Exchange of Singapore. Later, IFS, including its original parent ECICS, were bought by Phillip Securities in a reverse takeover. By then I had already left ECICS and IFS to hibernate in complete retirement. Or so I thought.

XVII

Afterlife 4: Neptune Orient Lines & Maritime Holdings

Neptune Orient Lines Ltd (NOL) was founded as a wholly government-owned company on the grounds that it would not be in the long-term strategic best interests of Singapore, as a leading shipping port in the region with entrepôt international connections, to not have at least one large shipping company of its own serving the main international shipping routes. This came to the fore when, just before the advent of container shipping and while break-bulk cargo shipping was still rife, the Far East Freight Conference held sway over shipping rates of the dominant service of the port of Singapore, to the UK. Singapore, with no major shipping company of its own on that and other international shipping routes, had no real say, nor influence, on shipping freight rates between the UK and Singapore or between Singapore and any other country's port. Even after NOL was newly founded and operational out of Singapore, it had to adopt a follow-the-leader stance in regard to freight rates.

I was appointed director to the Board of NOL in 1972 and later, when Deputy Chairman Low Guan Onn of Jurong Shipyard passed away, non-executive deputy chairman, while in full-time service of the government. In that capacity, my wife Peggy was invited by then NOL chairman, Michael Wong Pakshong, to accompany me to Ishikawa Harima Heavy Industries' Imabari Shipyard in Japan to launch an NOL Freedom-class newbuild. It was an exhilarating experience to see the champagne bottle, with guide ropes to ensure an accurate hit, smash against the bow of the vessel, and the champagne gush down into the belly of the slipway below. Then, to the wailing of the ship siren, the vessel slipped stern first down the slipway and into the deeper water outside. It was secured and towed back alongside the dock, to await its final fittings and then go on its sea trials before going fully operational. After the launching, Peggy and I were sent on a visit to Nikko, where the gold autumn leaves of the trees shimmered before cascading down and carpeting the ground below. A sight to behold! After which, Peggy and I were despatched by air, on a regular airline service from Tokyo Narita Airport, back to Singapore.

Later, when I was appointed non-executive chairman of NOL in 1984, I had to officiate at numerous container-ship launchings for NOL, performed by the wives of selected business associates of NOL and of other business and commercial VIPs, in Japan where the bulk of NOL's newbuilds originated from, and later South Korea. On one occasion, for an associate Indonesian shipping company of NOL, a couple of vessels were built at the Jiangnan Shipyard in Shanghai, which in its earlier life had been a Chinese naval dockyard. That was a most memorable launching. The NOL delegation was given the royal VIP treatment, following the launching, and we were housed in Beijing at the official Diaoyutai guest house, where Dr Goh Keng Swee happened also to be staying at the time, while on a separate mission to China, though we were in separate buildings within that large guest house compound. Our NOL delegation was escorted on a sightseeing tour in Beijing to the Forbidden City and Tiananmen Square, then on to the Ming Tombs and the Great Wall. And, later, also to Guilin for a day's cruise down the river to see the cormorants there, with rings around their throats, sent out from their fishermen's boats into the river to catch fish for their masters. Finally we went to Guangzhou,which my wife Peggy was especially pleased to visit since she herself descended from a Cantonese line, for an escorted tour, then by train across the border and into Hong Kong, from where the NOL delegation returned to Singapore. There was much feasting on delicacies during that sojourn, and many cups of Maotai to toasts of "Ganbei!"

But all was not feasting and wining. NOL fell on hard times, with freight rates on its services to and from the US much depressed, largely owing to over-capacity on that service. The US-controlled Carrier Act forced NOL to seek reduction in the government-owned shareholding in NOL from sixty to forty per cent. Then, seeking to position itself within the top six or so largest container shipping carriers in the world to give it sufficient leverage in the world shipping market, NOL set about purchasing the venerable American President Lines (APL) following a worldwide search by and recommendation of a leading financial institutional adviser that had been specifically commissioned by NOL for that very purpose. This, however, incidentally led to the query and interrogation of NOL's senior-most officers by counsel for the Securities & Exchange Commission of the US in New York for alleged insider trading in the purchase by a Singapore-registered company not related to NOL of a significant quantity of APL common stock before the deal was made public and common knowledge. The NOL CEO and CFO were with me at the time in the US for calls in Washington DC on the then

Chairperson of the Federal Maritime Commission in connection with NOL's intended purchase of APL, and on relevant congressmen to explain and clarify the objectives of the intended purchase. Then, on to lunch with the president of the trade union representing sea-going personnel to seek his union's in-principle support for the deal. All arranged by the adviser in the US whom NOL had been advised would be needed and whom NOL engaged for the whole deal to go through smoothly. An exciting and new exhilarating experience for me, learning how such deals got done in the US and its complicated systems in such matters where the to-know-whom seemed so crucial.

Back in Singapore, I reported to the Chairman of Temasek Holdings which had the controlling shareholding in NOL, on all that had transpired, in particular the encounter with the SEC and fallout from that, which did not make him too happy with NOL and especially its chairman: me. But the situation for NOL got worse. NOL was in the red to a large extent, with a big overhang of expensive short-term debt taken on essentially for the purchase of APL. The financial crisis of 1996/1997 had caused banks in Singapore – none of which could be asked to assure NOL in advance of any long-term financial support for NOL's purchase of APL, as the deal had to be and was done before NOL could even whisper about NOL's intended purchase – to reject outright at that time any long-term financial support for the purchase. NOL just had to soldier along, as best it could, with only short-term high-interest loans. With the bad situation that NOL was in at the time, and no apparent turn around for NOL then, the Chairman of Temasek very justifiably sought my departure as Chairman of NOL, which I readily agreed to and did not offer myself for re-election as Chairman of NOL at the latter's AGM that immediately followed. Thus came to an end my long saga in NOL, 1972 to 1999 – a quarter-century in all as director, deputy chairman and finally chairman.

Just when I was about to relinquish an earlier position as Executive Chairman of NOL and revert to non-executive chairman, I was offered appointment as Executive Chairman of Maritime Holdings through my good friend Goh Choo Keng, who had been both Director Marine, and Portmaster in Singapore before taking up an appointment on a couple of years' contract with a service company in Saudi Arabia owned by the founder and principal shareholder of Maritime Holdings. Captain Goh was then already in the employ of Maritime Holdings in Singapore. Maritime Holdings was essentially in the business of chartering tugboats out to mining companies in Indonesia, to tow fully laden barges downriver in remote Indonesia, essentially in Kalimantan, for their cargoes to be loaded onto ships, for transportation elsewhere. Then the empty barges were towed back up the river to their loading depots once more. On one visit to Indonesia with Goh Choo Keng to check on a mine in Kalimantan, we were flown in a helicopter up a mountainside. It appeared sometimes to me, as we flew up that mountainside, that we were headed straight into the side of that mountain. But we flew up and up, cleared the mountain and landed on the other side at the brim of a large opencast mine. There were bulldozers running around that open-pit mine, scooping the earth and loading it onto large trucks standing by, which then drove up the steep side of the deep mine pit on tracks cut into the side of the mine pit, with their engines screaming out in great strain. The trucks delivered their precious cargoes to the loading bays on the riverbank which was then carried from there in barges towed by the tugs downriver to be loaded onto ships and transported to places far away. My time in Maritime Holdings as chairman came to an end very soon. I had a falling out with its founder and principal shareholder, though we become friends again not long after that, before that founder and principal shareholder succumbed to cancer and passed away.

XVIII

Afterlife 5: Singapore Casket Company & The Eurasian Association

Singapore Casket Company Pte Ltd was jointly founded in 1920 by my grandfather, John Hochstadt, and his wife, Rosa Delphina née D'Almeida who grew it into a thriving funeral business and the largest of its kind in Singapore. My father, Henry David Hochstadt, had no interest at all in the business and much preferred to become a teacher after finishing school. My uncle, C B (Carlo) Webb, who married my father's elder sister, Marion (May), joined the business, initially as general manager, and later became managing director. He married another of my father's sisters, Grace, following the death of his first wife Marion. He thus inherited shares in the company, both directly from my grandfather and also from Marion and Grace, making him the largest shareholder in the company, some of which shares he passed on to his son, Augustus (Guy) Webb. When Carlo retired to Australia he left his shares to his son Guy, who was initially general manager, then managing director. Guy's shares went to his children including his son, Preston, who was then a manager in the company. Preston and his wife and family later migrated to Vancouver in British Columbia. Along the way, a French funeral company acquired shares in Singapore Casket Co and effectively became the single largest shareholder. My father, who had by then retired from the education service, was non-executive chairman of the company for a time before giving that up to retire completely. I was invited to become a non-executive director following my retirement from the Ministry of Law, which I accepted. The French company subsequently sold its shares to a US company that in turn later sold its shares to an Australian company, which then became in effect the largest single shareholder in Singapore Casket Co.

It was a novel experience for me sitting on the Board of Singapore Casket Co as a non-executive director through the company's transition from what it had been to what it became, with co-directors from France, the US and Australia helping guide the organisation through the changing business environment in Singapore and changes that particularly affected the funeral-related business. I learnt a lot. When the Australian company bought over Singapore Casket entirely, I used part of the money I got from selling my shares to make a substantial donation to the Eurasian Association of Singapore which, in turn, used part of that donation for the main meeting room on the second floor of the Eurasian Community House at 139 Ceylon Road, named the John Hochstadt Room in honour of my grandfather. The meeting room was officially opened by the President of Singapore, S R Nathan, who was then also patron of the Eurasian Association of Singapore.

The Eurasian Association of Singapore had a history going back to 1919 when it was founded just after World War I and as an indirect consequence of the latter. It was founded by Eurasians and, as it most proudly proclaimed, for Eurasians. It had a chequered history following 1919, of not being any too successful or active in its declared aims and objectives but, rather, falling into a Rip Van Winkle-like slumber. That is until Lieutenant Colonel Timothy De Souza of the RSAF took it upon himself to awaken the slumbering Eurasian Association (EA). He was the EA president, while Minister for Law Eddie Barker was the Minister responsible for Eurasian affairs in the Cabinet and became EA patron. A few other Singapore Eurasians, including me, were drafted as life trustees. Around then the government got going with its Self Help Groups, to help serve the developmental needs of each of the main ethnic groups in the overall Singapore population: CDAC for the Chinese, MENDAKI for the Malays and SINDA for the Indians. As for the Eurasians, with an estimated population of not even 16,000, they were considered by the government to be far too small in number and in proportion to the overall population to merit an official support body. At that time, the Eurasians of Singapore were not considered a strong enough community to even have their own category under the "Chinese, Malay, Indian, Others" official categorisation of Singaporeans. They were lumped into the "Others" category. It wasn't until later, after much argy-bargy and toing and froing between the EA, on the one hand, and the powers-that-be, on the other, that the categorisation was expanded to "Chinese, Malay, Indian, Eurasian, Others". Singapore's Eurasians rejoiced that they were no longer classified as "Others" but had then official recognition of their place as Singaporeans.

Largely through the efforts of the EA president, Timothy De Souza, and his hard-working management committee, the awakened Eurasian Association was entrusted by government to be the official Self Help Group for Singapore Eurasians, both complementary and supplementary to the association's original aims and objectives. This was a singular honour amongst the various ethnic-based registered associations and societies of Singapore, and likely a consequence of the relatively tiny Eurasian population. But the change in status put much pressure on the EA president and management committee to get things going and done, expeditiously. And that pressure, of course, in turn bore hard on the Life Trustees. The Trustees had a standing invitation to sit in on management committee meetings. Initially, the meetings were held in conference rooms borrowed from the Peoples' Association at the old Kallang Airport, and later, in a couple of adjacent single-storey bungalows on Mountbatten Road, which were once living quarters for expatriate British officers of the colonial government and their families, then on short-term lease to EA by the then Singapore Land Office. There the EA remained while approval was sought and obtained from the Ministry of Finance for public funds to be allocated to the EA to lease land from the government at 139 Ceylon Road on a long-term basis. At Ceylon Road was to be built the Eurasian Community House, across the road from the private residence of the then President of Singapore, S R Nathan, and family. President Nathan was also appointed a patron of the Eurasian Association.

When the new premises were up and ready for occupation, the EA moved in. It was the very first time in its near 100-year existence that the EA was fortunate enough to have its very own purpose-built premises. As representative of the extended Hochstadt family, I had received from the new owners of Singapore Casket Co a marble bust each of my grandfather John Hochstadt, joint founder and one-time chairman of the company, and of the latter's son-in-law and later managing director, Carlo Webb. The busts had stood in Singapore Casket Co's office premises at 129/133 Lavender Street. I, in turn, passed them on to then EA vice president, Dr Barry Pereira, who had been entrusted with setting up the "John Hochstadt Room" and who arranged for the marble bust of my grandfather to be mounted on a stand at its entrance. A photograph of my grandfather and grandmother, John and Rosa Delphina Hochstadt, selected by then EA vice president, Dr Barry Pereira, was displayed on a wall inside that room, together with a few photos from the Hochstadt family photo album. As for the marble bust of my uncle Carlo, the general manager of EA, Lester Low, assured me that it would go into the store at the EA Community House for safekeeping, pending possible later display in an exhibition on Singapore Eurasian contribution, largely by way of the Eurasian contingent of the Singapore Volunteer Corps (SVC), to the war effort in World War II. My Uncle Carlo Webb, having served as a mobilised captain in the Eurasian contingent of the SVC and sent to work on the infamous Siam-Burma Death Railway, which he survived, and later upon demobilisation, was promoted to the rank of major.

Following the demise of former Minister for Law Eddie Barker, then EA President Brian Davenport appointed me EA patron, in addition to being a life trustee. Sometime following the reclassification of "life trustees" as "trustees", I stepped down to make way for a new EA trustee. I continued to serve as patron, concurrently with S R Nathan and former Minister George Yeo. Upon the demise of the former, George Yeo and I remained as the EA's only patrons.

As patron of the Eurasian Association of Singapore my earnest prayer in its 100th year in 2019, was that the EA venture into fresh fields and pastures new in furtherance of its original aims and objectives and, over and above that, help to maintain and further the tolerant, harmonious and peaceful development of the Republic of Singapore and all its peoples. The membership of the association being admirably suited for that purpose, because within the wider Eurasian community of Singapore is the DNA of the principal ethnic, cultural, and religious milieu of the entire population of the Republic of Singapore.

XIX
Epilogue

The story of the Hochstadts in Singapore began when Philip Peter or Peter Philip Hochstadt somehow, for reasons unknown, found his way to British India where he married a fiery red-haired Irish-Indian, Elizabeth, whose temper matched her fiery hair and the fiery chilli-hot curries that she once dished out in a home meal to a young friend of the family, who shouted out in dismay, "They eat fire! They eat fire!" Philip Peter or Peter Philip then appeared to have wandered around in Southeast Asia with family in tow. His son John Hochstadt, my grandfather, born in Kuching, Sarawak of the Rajah Brookes, retired early from the sea, on which he served as marine engineer in those early days of the steamship, rising to chief engineer on board SS *Muar*, plying the coastal trade.

Following retirement from the sea, John Hochstadt jointly founded Singapore Casket Company Pte Ltd in 1920 with wife Rosa Delphina, granddaughter of the famed Dr Sir Jose D'Almeida in the days or thereabouts of Thomas Stamford Raffles. John and Rosa Delphina Hochstadt's children were Annie, whose husband Vickery fell into a tank of hot, just smelted tin ore while working at a Straits Trading smelting plant, and perished tragically; Flora, who divorced her first husband, an Englishman named Pattinson, and later married Dutch Dirk van Vliet and ran a boarding house on Grange Road; Marion (May) who married Carlo Webb, the general manager and later managing director of Singapore Casket Co who later retired to Queensland, Australia, to live out his days with his daughter Pearl; Cornelia (Nellie), who married Captain Frederick Jannings; Grace, who married Carlo Webb as his second wife following the death of Marion from cancer; surviving son Henry David who married Beryl Lucy (Girlie) Phillips; youngest daughter Alice; and eldest son Victor who succumbed to tuberculosis in his twenties, rife in those days and often fatal.

Singapore Casket Co grew to became a premier provider of funerals, memorials and related services in Singapore and beyond. Associate companies owned and run by members of the extended family were set up in Malaya. Young Henry David had no desire to follow in the footsteps of his father. After finishing his schooling at St Joseph's Institution on Bras Basah Road he became a teacher, rising to school principal and to inspector, then to Chief Inspector of Schools before retiring at age fifty-five as Assistant Director of Education in the Ministry of Education at Kay Siang Road. Henry David married Beryl Lucy (Girlie) Phillips, only daughter of Captain John Phillips of Liverpool and his wife Helen Marcus.

John and Helen Phillips had three sons, all elder to their only daughter Girlie: John Junior (Sonny) who became an audit assistant; Arthur who became a teacher; and Stanley Walter who was a marine engineer, then superintendent of the Shell Company on Pulau Bukom, which then housed one of the largest oil installations in the world. John Phillips, a British national, was interned as POW during the Japanese Occupation of Singapore. He died during internment, following a fall after surgery for acute appendicitis, in the POW ward of Singapore General Hospital. His wife Helen was interned only in the last few months of the war even though she was then paralysed from a stroke. She died a short while after. Their eldest son Sonny was not interned during the occupation, owing to being lame in one leg as a result of a bad bout of rheumatic fever that he had suffered in his youth. Arthur and Stanley Walter were also interned, very soon after their father. Girlie was spared internment through appeal by her husband Henry David Hochstadt to and personal intervention of then Japanese Civilian Administrator, Mamoru Shinozaki, owing to her being married to my father Henry David, officially shown on his birth certificate as German, born of a German father, my paternal grandfather John Hochstadt.

I went to the Japanese Ceylon Road Boys' School during the Japanese Occupation of Singapore, which they renamed Syonan-to or Light of The East Island: Ceylon Road Boys' School was an afternoon session school at pre-World War II St Hilda's Girls' School, and later to Koon Seng Road Boys' School, previously Presbyterian Boys School, when enrolment at Ceylon Road Boys' School fell too low. Every morning at Koon Seng Road Boys' School we had to sing "Kimigayo", the Japanese national anthem, in tune to the morning broadcast blared out from an old valve radio set, while standing to attention and facing the Japanese national flag of the Rising Sun. Then we would do Radio Taisho stretch exercises, to tunes from the small radio on stage, to the count of eight: ichi, ni, san, shi, goh, roku, sichi, hachi!

Following the Japanese Occupation of Singapore from 1942 to 1945, I lived through British re-occupation, then through Singapore's own life as an internally self-governed state under overall British dominance, on to Singapore as a state of Malaysia with the brief interlude from 31 August 1963 to formation of Malaysia on 15 September 1963 as a unilaterally declared independent state, and finally in the independent Republic of Singapore.

Beginning with Singapore as a Crown Colony of Great Britain, I had to stand to attention pre World War II while facing the Union Jack and sing "God Save The King"; then stand to attention while facing the Rising Sun flag of the Japanese conquerors and sing "Kimigayo"; and stand to attention facing the Union Jack while singing "God Save the King" once more; and again stand to attention facing the Union Jack but sing "God Save the Queen" that time; then stand to attention while facing the freshly designed red and white flag of the State of Singapore with crescent and stars, while singing out loud "Majullah Singapura"; then stand to attention, facing the Malaysian flag while singing the one-time Federation of Malaya and then Malaysian anthem, "Negara Ku"; and lastly, stand to attention facing the crescent and stars of the red and white flag of the Republic of Singapore while once again, singing loud and clear for the high heavens to hear, "Majullah Singapura"! All the while in only one and the same place: Singapore!

Curriculum Vitae of Herman Ronald Hochstadt

Biographical Summary

Herman Ronald Hochstadt (hrh), a Singapore citizen, was born in Singapore on 19 May 1933 and completed his primary and secondary school education at St Andrew's School, Singapore. He graduated from the then University of Malaya in Singapore with a BA (Honours) in 1958. An alumnus of INSEAD in Fontainebleau, France, which he attended on a French government grant in 1978 to undertake the Stanford–INSEAD Advanced Management Programme, he was a US State Department Distinguished Visitor in 1974 and elected Fellow of the Management Development Institute of Singapore in 1976 and of the Singapore Institute of Management in 1988. He was elected to the Board of Governors of the Asian Institute of Management in the Philippines from 1989 to 1994 and was awarded the following Singapore National Day Awards: Public Administration Medal (Bronze) 1963, Public Administration Medal (Gold) 1978 and Public Service Star 1998.

He served as Non-Resident High Commissioner to Botswana, Mauritius, Namibia, South Africa, Swaziland and Tanzania from 1989 to 1999 and was also appointed Special Envoy to Kenya, Malawi, Mauritius, Mozambique, Swaziland, Tanzania, Uganda and Zimbabwe from 1998 to 2000. He was appointed to the

Presidential Council for Minority Rights from 1989 to 2010 and to the Presidential Election Committee in 1993, 1999 and 2005 and to the Board of Governors of the Singapore International Foundation from 1991 to 2001 and to the Inland Revenue Authority of Singapore from 1992 to 2000, as well as Special Adviser to the Maritime and Ports Authority of Singapore from 1998 to 2000. He was a Pro-Chancellor of Nanyang Technological University in Singapore from 1995 to 2016, patron and life trustee of the Eurasian Association of Singapore and trustee of Ang Moh Kio Community Hospital in Singapore.

Herman Hochstadt retired from the Singapore senior civil service in 1989 after having served in various positions in several Ministries and statutory authorities since 1959, including the Prime Minister's Office, Ministry of Finance, Ministry of Foreign Affairs, Ministry of Interior & Defence, Monetary Authority of Singapore and the Board of Commissioners of Currency, Singapore and as Permanent Secretary in the Ministries of Communications, Education, Finance and Law. He was chairman of the former Singapore Telephone Board, Telecommunication Authority of Singapore and Provisional Mass Rapid Transit Authority and also served as a member of the Economic Development Board, Central Provident Fund Board, Port of Singapore Authority, National Productivity Board, Adult Education Board, Vocational and Industrial Training Board and the Mass Rapid Transit Corporation. He was chairman of Singapore Turf Club from 1994 to 2001.

He was on the boards of the former Malaysia Singapore Airlines and Morgan Guaranty & Partners, and of Singapore Airlines, Neptune Orient Lines, ECICS Holdings, Temasek Holdings, International Factors (Singapore), Cycle & Carriage, Singapore Reinsurance Corporation, Maritime Holdings, Thakral Corporation, Parkway Holdings, Raffles Holdings and AV Jennings of Australia among others. He was on the Board of Singapore Casket Company from 1991 to 2016.

Herman Hochstadt is a widower with a daughter Karen Lynn and son, Erwin Wei-Sung. His late wife, Peggy Leong Wai Chee, was chief librarian of National University of Singapore.

Appointments (Public Service)

1.	1959–1962	Assistant Secretary, Ministry of Finance
2.	1962–1965	Secretary to Prime Minister, Prime Minister's Office
3.	1965	Principal Assistant Secretary, Ministry of Foreign Affairs
4.	1965–1967	Director of Manpower, Ministry of Interior & Defence
5.	1967–1968	Principal Assistant Secretary, Ministry of Foreign Affairs
6.	1968–1969	Principal Assistant Secretary, Ministry of Finance
7.	1969–1972	Deputy Secretary, Ministry of Finance
8.	1972–1975	Permanent Secretary, Ministry of Communications
9.	1976–1980	Permanent Secretary, Ministry of Education
10.	1980–1981	Deputy Managing Director (Special Duties), Monetary Authority of Singapore
11.	1981–1982	General Manager, Board of Commissioners of Currency, Singapore
12.	1981–1984	Permanent Secretary, Ministry of Finance (Budget Division)
13.	1984–1986	Permanent Secretary, Ministry of Finance (Budget Division) and concurrently Ministry of Law

14.	1987–1989	Permanent Secretary, Ministry of Law
15.	1989–1994	High Commissioner (Non-Resident) to Mauritius & Tanzania
16.	1992–1994	Special Representative to South Africa
17.	1995–2000	High Commissioner (Non-Resident) to South Africa
18.	1995–1999	High Commissioner (Non-Resident) to Namibia
19.	1995–2000	High Commissioner (Non-Resident) to Botswana
20.	1995–1999	High Commissioner (Non-Resident) to Swaziland
21.	1998	Special Envoy to Tanzania, Mauritius, Zimbabwe, Mozambique and Malawi
22.	1999–2000	Special Envoy to Kenya, Tanzania and Uganda

Appointments (Companies & Statutory Authorities)

1.	1969–1971	Board Member, Central Provident Fund
2.	1971–1973	Board Member, Economic Development Board
3.	1971–1977	Director, ACMA Electrical Industries
4.	1971–1972	Board Member, Malaysia – Singapore Airlines
5.	1971–1972	Executive Council Member, Singapore Institute of Management
6.	1972–1985	Director, Singapore Airlines
7.	1972–1999	Director & Chairman, Neptune Orient Lines Ltd and Companies in NOL Group including APL

8.	1972–1975	Chairman, Bus Services Licensing Authority
9.	1972–1975	Board Member, Port of Singapore Authority
10.	1973–1974	Chairman, Singapore Telephone Board
11.	1973–1974	Chairman, Telecommunication Authority of Singapore
12.	1973–1979	Director, Morgan Guaranty & Partners
13.	1976–1979	Chairman, Governing Board of South East Asian Ministers of Education Organisation (SEAMEO) Regional Language Centre
14.	1978–1979	Board Member, Adult Education Board
15.	1978–1980	Deputy Chairman, Vocational & Industrial Training Board
16.	1980–1999	Chairman, ECICS Holdings
17.	1980–1981	Chairman, Singapore Clearing House Association
18.	1980–1983	Chairman, Provisional Mass Rapid Transit Authority
19.	1981–1982	Director, Singapore Mint
20.	1981–1992	Director, Temasek Holdings
21.	1981–1983	Member, National Productivity Council
22.	1982	Member, National Wages Council
23.	1983–1986	Board Member, Mass Rapid Transit Corporation
24.	1987–1995	Chairman, International Factors and Companies in IFS Group
25.	1989–2010	Member, Presidential Council for Minority Rights
26.	1989–1993	Director, Cycle & Carriage and Companies in CCL Group
27.	1989–1994	Director, Singapore Reinsurance Corporation

28.	1989–1994	Director, ACMA
29.	1989–1991	Chairman, Inno Pacific Holdings
30.	1989–1995	Chairman, APR International Loss Adjusters & Surveyors
31.	1989–2010	Member, Presidential Council for Minority Rights
32.	1991 – 1995	Chairman, Maritime Holdings and Companies in Maritime Group
33.	1991–2016	Director, Singapore Casket Company
34.	1991–2001	Member, Board of Governors, Singapore International Foundation
35.	1991–1993	Director, Dowty Aerospace Engineering
36.	1992–2000	Member, Inland Revenue Authority of Singapore
37.	1993	Member, Presidential Elections Committee
38.	1994–2001	Chairman, Singapore Turf Club
39.	1994–1995	Director, China Walden Venture Investments
40.	1995–2015	Pro-Chancellor, Nanyang Technological University
41.	1995	Director, Gateway Transport Company (Myanmar)
42.	1995–2000	Vice-Chairman, Thakral Corporation
43.	1997–1999	Chairman, APL & Companies in the Group
44.	1998–2000	Special Adviser, Maritime & Ports Authority of Singapore
45.	1998–2000	Director, Parkway Holdings
46.	1999–2001	Director, Raffles Holdings
47.	1999	Member, Presidential Elections Committee
48.	2005	Member, Presidential Elections Committee

Singapore National Day Awards

1.	1963	Public Administration Medal (Bronze)
2.	1978	Public Administration Medal (Gold)
3.	1998	Public Service Star

Other Honours & Awards

1.	1974	US State Department Distinguished Visitor
2.	1976	Fellow, Management Development Institute of Singapore
3.	1988	Fellow, Singapore Institute of Management
4.	2011	Distinguished Member, NUS Society
5.	2015	Distinguished Arts and Social Sciences Alumni Award, NUS
6.	2019	Distinguished Alumni Service Award, NUS

National University of Singapore's
Faculty of Arts & Social Sciences
Annual Dinner and Dance 1988
29 January 1988

For NATIONAL UNIVERSITY OF SINGAPORE'S FACULTY OF ARTS & SOCIAL SCIENCES ANNUAL DINNER & DANCE 1988
29 JANUARY 1988

On behalf of my wife, Peggy, and myself, I thank you for the honour of being invited as your guests-of-honour tonight. I do not really know why this honour was bestowed on me. I would have much preferred the unmitigated pleasure of merely coming here tonight as an ordinary guest accompanying the Chief Librarian to wine, dine and enjoy the company. Instead I have now to speak for, so I was politely told in a letter, some 20 minutes. But, I was warned in the letter, also very politely, that this is an informal gathering so, presumably, what I am to say should be informal too. Being a civil servant of near to 30 years under the guiding hand of the Instruction Manuals and standing and ad hoc instructions, and not being so used to public speaking as to internal minuting, I find it difficult to speak, let alone speak in public for some 20 minutes. And to such an august gathering, though informal, I could possibly, speak quite knowledgeably and authoritatively for that length of time on the Government Instruction Manuals. But, that would not go down too well with the good food and drink, I fear.

Since minuting suits me better, I have penned a somewhat lengthy, for me, prosaic piece which, if read slowly enough, could take the better part of the prescribed time. In the sometime manner of Sir Humphrey Appleby, however, it may not mean any too much.

2. In trying to decide what to minute on to read to you tonight that might have some semblance of relevance, I thought it would be useful to first try to establish why I was asked to be guest-of-honour. I am not even a graduate of the NUS proper. I am only a graduate of one of its predecessors, the original University of Malaya, and not a particularly outstanding one at that. Maybe it is because Dean Thumboo's friendship with me goes a long way back to the days of the Bukit Timah campus of the then University of Malaya of more than 30 years ago. This friendship continued into the time when he graduated into an income tax officer (before he got involved with the CPF, telephones and became an academic) and I was still a rather impecunious student at the University. But I did have an old second-hand motor-cycle on which he occasionally wanted a ride to and from the

University library to look up some obscure book on ancient Eastern folklore or some such as background material for some even more obscure poem he was contemplating. In recompense, he took me equally occasionally to curry lunch at the original Gomez on Mount Sophia. I guess, having run out of suitable invitees as guest-of-honour for tonight, Prof Thumboo decided to call on those old memories again and knew I would buckle to the pressure of his thumb. Or maybe Prof Thumboo, in a Shakespearean bent, felt that a little comic relief might be right following the tragedy of the crash after the previous address to you by my erstwhile civil service colleague and current Singapore Stock Exchange Chairman. Indeed, Prof Thumboo did remark to someone that I could be expected to bring in some wry humour.But I'm not too sure whether he was referring to "rye".

3. I decided in the end to write this minute to try to span the reading space of the prescribed time with some reminiscing. Having been nearly 30 years in the civil service, it is tempting to reminisce on work and life in the civil service which in my case, spans 7 Ministries, including the Prime Minister's Office, and

a statutory board. I may add that I have never been in Labour. A rolling stone, they say, gathers no moss which may be true but I've gathered some stories on the civil service. Over the last few years, I've had regular annual visits to my office arranged by the Law Faculty for groups of law students of the NUS who ostensibly want to learn something of the workings of the Ministry and its departments. Usually after some rather innocuous questioning, they get down to questions about the relationship between the Minister and his Permanent Secretary. They hope, I'm sure, to hear something in the mode of Sir Humphrey Appleby of "Yes Minister" and "Yes Prime Minister" fame. I've had to disappoint them. And I must disappoint you too tonight should you be expecting some reminiscing in like vein. Such will have to await my retirement from the civil service which should not be too far hence. Perhaps then, I may have something to offer my friend who is now directing policy studies to lighten the weight of that burden and to help fill my time and allow me to earn enough to replace the many golf balls I keep losing.

4. I shall venture now, instead, into a little reminiscing on what I have already touched on in my introductory remarks - the NUS and its predecessors. There is a special uniqueness about this University. A person could, theoretically at least, have a diploma from the former Raffles College, a bachelor's degree from the University of Malaya, a master's degree from the previous University of Singapore and a doctorate from the National University of Singapore and yet be deemed to have been to only one institution of higher learning. This evolution of the NUS has taken place within the comparatively short time of a slightly extended undergraduate to postgraduate lifetime of a normal student. The NUS administrators may want to look up the registers to see how close anyone has actually come to achieving graduation from the Raffles College through to the NUS, and bestow some special honour.

5. In the final years of my secondary school in the late 1940s, there was much news of setting up a university to serve both Singapore and the then

Malaya. This led to establishment of the original University of Malaya which took in the former Raffles College catering to the Arts and Sciences and the King Edward VII College of Medicine. In school, many of us contributed our little donation of a few dollars in exchange for pieces of paper symbolising the bricks of the great new university to be built. A site was to be designated in Johore, so as to better serve Malaya and Singapore. There was much enthusiasm for the new university from the public at large but essentially the English educated. This enthusiasm was nowhere near that, however, generated by the proposed establishment of the Nanyang University not so much later. I have never seen such a jam of traffic and people all bent on a common destination as there was at the official opening of Nanyang University. I remember getting out of our car which was stuck in a mass of stationary vehicles of all kinds some miles from the destination and trudging with my fellow University student union councillors to the Nanyang campus. We arrived there in near darkness, hours after the appointed time. Thousands of people were still around just gazing at the wonder and taking in the flavour.

6. There was a great debate in the English language newspapers of the day at the time when the original University of Malaya was being established as to whether honorary degrees should be awarded by the university. There were several English language newspapers then - apart from the Straits Times there were the Malaya Tribune, the Singapore Standard and a Singapore Free Press. This controversy about honorary degrees seems somehow to have been resolved and the original University of Malaya did award honorary degrees as did its successors and does the NUS.

7. By the time I did get into the then University of Malaya at the Bukit Timah campus housing the Faculties of Arts and Sciences in the early 50s, the question of a site in Johore for the great new university to be built for Singapore and Malaya also seemed to have fizzled out. The University of Malaya appeared set to continue life vigorously at Bukit Timah with the Arts and Science Faculties and at Sepoy Lines with the Medical and Dental Faculties. Perhaps a reason for the fading away of the Johore vision was

the Emergency which was then still at a high point with Johore being one of the most affected states of Malaya. Anyway, with the fading of the vision, we were left holding those pieces of paper but with no bricks to touch or point to. Perhaps your VC would now designate some bricks at Kent Ridge for us. The active canvassing of donations large and small from the public for the foundation of the original University of Malaya and the Nanyang University demonstrates the extent of the public support for and empathy with a university that can be generated. I'm sure the VC will agree it beats the support and empathy that may arise from budget meetings with MOF officials on university subventions.

8. Life was much simpler in those early days of the orginal University of Malaya for the academic administrators. There were no Social Sciences as such. The Arts Faculty only offered English Literature, Mathematics, Economics, History and Geography as degree subjects. The total student enrolment numbered about one quarter of the total student intake for a single year now in the NUS. A student in any of the Faculties of the University then could probably recognise by

sight one third or more of the entire student enrolment and name perhaps some 10 or 20 per cent . A walk through the quadrangle at Bukit Timah, which was a popular shortcut, once or more a day gave the opportunity over a student lifetime to encounter almost the entire student population of the Arts and Science Faculties. Even many medical and dental students (there was no Engineering and Architecture then) would be encountered on these walks. English Language was a first year subject in the Arts Faculty and had to be taken by all first year Science and Medical and Dentistry students. This smallness and closeness engendered great camaraderie which is apparent even today amongst the senior echelons of the civil services of Singapore and Malaysia who were contemporaries in the original University of Malaya and recognise each other from old when they meet.

9. There were clear distinctions then, as must be now, between classes of students. There were the Arts and Science students and the Medicos. Each regarded the other as somewhat inferior. There was intense rivalry between the Faculties at Bukit Timah and those

at Sepoy Lines, especially in sports. The inter-faculty rugger matches in particular could be rather bloody both on field and off. Then there were the Hostellites and the Non-Hostellites. The Hostellites generally regarded themselves as the leaders of and great participants in student union and university social and cultural life. The Non-Hostellites they looked down on as apathetic bookworms capable only of finding their way to and from the lecture room, the library, the canteen for lunch or dinner and home, without the ability to even get the quorums for their own NHO or Non-Hostellites Organisation. As the owner of a motor-cycle and able and willing to provide occasional and speedy transportation, I was in the happy status of enjoying hostel life for a considerable proportion of any student life as a non-official hostellite. Until, however, the Master spotted me one evening as I was coming out of the shower with a towel around my waist. All that provision of transportation to fellow undergraduates and occasional graduates, must have stood me in some stead. In later working life I had to serve in the Ministry of Communications and look after land, sea and air transportation amongst other responsibilities. I even came to sit on the authority set up to see to the establishment of the MRT.

10. There was much political and social ferment and turmoil in Singapore and Malaya in those days of the original University of Malaya. The University was not spared. Student political activism in the Chinese Middle Schools was strident and there was some in the University too, but of varying degrees of idealism, fervour and revolutionary zeal. Prof Thumboo, I am sure will recall, that while he was still an undergraduate, some students were woken early one morning in the hostel at Dunearn Road by the then colonial Special Branch. They were associated with the University of Malaya Socialist Club and its publication, "Fajar". "Fajar" means Dawn in Malay, so maybe it was appropriate that the Special Branch came at dawn. I myself a few years later was elected to the Central Working Committee of the University of Malaya Socialist Club as Publications Secretary. Fortunately or unfortunately, the Club had by then lost its licence to publish for some time and I never brought out a single issue during my tenure of office. Several visits were

made to Robinson Road to see a particularly knotty colonial gentleman named Knott who was Archivist in the Special Branch and whose approval was needed to restore the licence. But to no avail.

11. The Chinese Middle School riots and Hock Lee Bus riots also took place during this time. During the height of one of these riots, a headless body was found strewn one morning at the foot of an embankment bordering the drive leading from Bukit Timah Road to the Bukit Timah campus. This body later proved to be that of a watchman at a construction site on campus who had been decapitated in a love triangle affair.

12. Not all was strife and turmoil, mayhem and murder on campus and its environs then. The Raffles Society devoted to the Arts and Literature flourished and actively published its "Cauldron", which was a hotch-potch of creative and not so creative contributions, then died out. The Society was revived some years later with a "New Cauldron". In the interim,there was the intense nationalism in Malaya

preceding the formation of the independent Federation of Malaya and after. There was much debate in the University as to the proper language for creative literary works and a serious proposal for Engmalchin, standing for a combination of English, Malay and Chinese. This was strenously debated and even attemptingly used. Years later, a similar debate flourished in the "New Cauldron" and a short-lived student publication called "Write" which Lloyd Fernando, formerly Professor of English at the new University of Malaya in Kuala Lumpur and my then fellow student in the Department of Philosophy in the original University of Malaya here, jointly founded and funded with me. The debate was to whether in Singapore and Malaya creative literary works in English should use the literally transliterated constructions of spoken local dialect sentences, for instance, or whether the equivalent of "proper" English idiom should be used. There were numerous other student publications of various sorts at the time all fired by great zeal and enthusiasm but little money, including the first volume of poems by a student at the University ever to be published. This was the "Rib of Earth" by Edwin Thumboo which was published and funded entirely through voluntary student effort.

13. There was also the lighter side or relief to student life with the usual sort of pranks that students get up to. Amongst the most memmorable to me were two perpetrated during a visit to the then Colony of Singapore by Prince Philip of Great Britain. The first was when the Prince's motorcade was expected along Dunearn Road and the traffic police were out in force along the road to control traffic. Other police stood by to provide security in especial conspicuity outside the Dunearn Road Hostel. An open convertible Morris Minor belonging to a student was decked out in appropriate regalia. A tall and slim student approximating as best possible the Prince's height, build and colouring in a borrowed military uniform stood in the back of the open car behind the driver who was another student in a borrowed chauffeur's uniform. The car was surreptitiously manoeuvred onto Dunearn Road and driven along the length of the road with the student Prince waving to the police and the people who had gathered to watch the real Prince Philip. The people waved back cheerily. The second was when a school and uniformed groups display was on at the Padang for Prince Philip to view from the City Hall. A

rather ragged-looking bunch of students in shorts and T-shirts of different styles and colours lumbered from seemingly nowhere on field in file during a brief lull in the programme. They proceeded to give a most uncoordinated display of arm, leg and body movements and then quickly disappeared into the crowd. There was utter consternation among the officials in charge of the display and the bigwigs present. But the real Prince seemed to enjoy it heartily.

14. Some of the pranks brought their own retribution. Like the April's Fool Flower Pot Caper. Late in the night on the eve of an April's Fool Day, a small bunch of students found their way into the long since closed for the day Central Library at Bukit Timah. They placed decorative plants in flower pots collected from around the buildings and quadrangle on each of the tables in the reading areas. Next morning when the library staff and students went into the library they were greeted by this colourful April's Fool display of plants. It was a mystery as to how the plants in their pots had got into the library although there was strong suspicion as to who was responsible.

The night watchman had seen the bunch of students around there late that night but not caught them in the act. There was also the suspicion that one of the students in the bunch had quietly unlatched one of the windows just before library closing time so that they could gain access through that window later. The same student or another, it was surmised, had gone to the library early next morning to catch the opening time and relatch the window before anyone could discover it had been unlatched. Nevertheless, since these were mere suspicions, though circumstantially strong, there was no retribution. But some years later when one of the perpetrators of the prank was a young married officer in the civil service smarting under a severe general pay-cut and able only to keep a single small second-hand car to be shared with his wife, who was then a probationary librarian in the University central library at Bukit Timah, he had to drive her to and from work. As a probationary librarian, the wife had to perform night duties on roster. The first time he went to pick her up after one of those night duties, he complained about the length of time he had had to wait outside the library for her to come out after closing time. She retorted that it could not be helped. Since the April's Fool Flower Pot Caper of some years earlier, the professional library staff on night duty had to go round to check each window to ensure they were securely latched before locking up the library.

15. In the evolution of the University, there was a time when it appeared there was a throwback to the ancestry of the Raffles and Medical Colleges. There was a University of Malaya in Kuala Lumpur and a University of Malaya in Singapore with a Principal as the administrative head of the latter sitting in the old Oei Tiong Ham Block. Some students in some Faculties spent some years in Kuala Lumpur and others years in Singapore. Some academic staff were shuttled to and fro like travelling salesmen or, perhaps I should say, salespersons. There seemed to be much confusion then in the University, and uncertainty.

16. In my later years at the University and the closer we got to 1959 and internal self-government for Singapore, there seemed to be a growing seriousness and purposefulness about student life, at least at Bukit

Timah. This may be because I myself had grown out of undergraduate life and had become what was then termed a Graduate Assistant. As a Graduate Assistant, I had to take on some tutoring. The tutoring included teaching formal logic to 1st Year Law students. To what practical purpose I did not then nor even later really know. I also had a group of outrageous but personally likeable Arts undergraduates to tutor in philosophy of no particular reputation as serious students. One was known to all as Alley Oop after a comic strip character of the day, whom he was said to resemble in looks and personality. They kept borrowing but never returning my cigarettes, both during tutorials and outside. On the $400 per month I was then expected to live on as a Graduate Assistant, it was increasingly difficult to survive and maintain myself and them on cigarettes. One day I switched to a pipe. Everyone in the group turned up for the next tutorial carrying a pipe each but no tobacco.

17. One night in 1959 soon after the first general election under full internal self-government for

Singapore, some students removed a large wooden name-board bearing the name of Prof Kiang Ai Kim from the campus and carted it off to Empress Place. They climbed with it up the statue of Raffles and planted it in the folded arms of the latter under the watchful but rather perplexed gaze of the armed Gurkha guards watching over the old Treasury vaults. The next morning the statue was the object of curious stares. Word went round that in like manner of the recent renaming of the Raffles Library and Museum as the National Library and National Museum, the statue of Raffles had apparently been renamed Prof Kiang Ai Kim.

18. The years between full internal self-government for Singapore and the merger of Singapore into Malaysia saw some very vociferous and strident political debate on campus which was even carried outside the campus and on the recently introduced television. Some of the most senior leaders of Government participated. There was also the continued evolution of the University with establishment of the University of Singapore quite distinct and separate from its sibling in Kuala Lumpur.

19. My stint as a tutor teaching logic to Law students led to my being called up for tutorial reservist service some years after I had left the University and entered the civil service. An apparent shortage of staff in the Philosophy Department and the need for someone to teach logic to 1st Year Law students led to my being called on to teach part-time. I still failed to see the purpose of teaching Formal Logic to Law students and told my students so but also said that since they were required to study it and I to teach it and was being paid to do so, we had best get on with the job. However, not long before their final 1st Year examinations, I had suddenly to go on civil service duty overseas for an extended period of about 2 months following the separation of Singapore from Malaysia and had to leave those 1st Year Law students in the lurch. What became of them in their logic examination, I did not know. I was not called again to do any part-time teaching. Recently, when I had to speak to a practising lawyer of some years concerning his nomination for a statutory appointment, he remarked that he was in that logic class. He seemed none the worse for it. Maybe my teaching of logic to 1st Year Law students in the past

has something to do with my present assignment in the civil service to the Ministry of Law.

20. The question of relevance of what is taught in the university, especially in the Arts and Social Sciences, to working life is one that comes up often. In fact, it was suggested that I could perhaps speak tonight about this, particularly in regard to the civil service. I would find it very difficult to speak on this and more so for the prescribed 20 minutes. I believe there is hardly any direct relevance. Subjects taught in the Arts and Social Sciences Faculty are not really vocational in the sense that Engineering, Medicine and Dentistry or Law may be. The question of their direct relevance should not arise. In my case, the direct relevance is even more questionable. For my first degree at the University of Malaya, I took English Literature, Pure Mathematics and Philosophy. I do not think there are any of my former university teachers here tonight to take umbrage at these remarks except possibly for Malcolm Wicks. Malcolm, I am sure, will not disagree and would not take it as a slur on his teaching or subject. The oddity of my combination

of English Literature, Pure Mathematics and Philosophy is such that, I am told, for about 20 years no one else attempted it. The daughter of a cousin of mine came to do it. The oddity may really be in the genes. For my Honours Degree, I took Philosophy through the grace of the University authorities who changed a rule specially to allow me to enter the first Philosophy Honours class in the University even though I had only offered Philosophy as a Subsidiary subject for my General Degree. But what is the direct relevance of Philosophy any more than English Literature or Pure Mathematics to what I am doing or have been doing for the last 30 years or so in the civil service? The relevance, if any, is not apparent to me. For Formal Logic it appears there may now be some use in the field of software engineering. For other subjects taught in the Arts and Social Science Faculties there may be some direct relevance to the working environment outside the university to varying degrees but not significantly, I believe.

21. I have come across bank managers who say that when they recruit trainees from amongst fresh

graduates, they do not care what subjects the recruits have taken in university so long as they can speak and write reasonably good English, are intelligent and numerate. The vocational skills and knowledge can be filled in on the job, complemented by special training programmes. This, of course, does not apply to specialist bank officers such as in the Economics and Research or Legal departments. It does not mean, however, that graduates of the English Department of the University are assured of generalist bank jobs. I have come across graduates in English Literature in the civil service who write the most Sir Humphreyish of confusing minutes and not by intent.

22. Between the University of Singapore stage and the present NUS, there was of course the stage of the joint campus with the former Nanyang University with which many of you are, I am sure, very familiar. Probably more so than me. The present NUS, therefore, has a natural kin of the same ancestry in the current University of Malaya and an adopted one in the Nanyang Technological Institute.

23. I have rambled on reminiscingly to your probable utter boredowm and consternation as to when I will end and you can get on with the serious business of wining and dining. So I will come to a conclusion. Minutes, I have been taught in the civil service and its training institutes, should come to a conclusion, especially the most lengthy ones. The conclusion should preferably make some succinct point or carry a message. What may be seen to have run through my rambling is that our University has gone through some not considerable transition and transformation in a relatively short span of time. There has been some loss of previous identity each time . The original University was founded in a spirit of some enthusiasm and fervour. This could still be tapped to the ultimate benefit of the University and society at large. I am often amazed at the tenacity with which some prominent American universities pursue their graduates long after the latter have left, to maintain the link. Our former Guild of Graduates, though a very tenuous link, has gone to dust. It should not be too much to keep in reasonable touch with the graduates on the register of the University and its antecedents

going right back to the Raffles and King Edward VII Medical Colleges. Opportunities for nostalgic get-togethers when the hostels at the old University campuses and the compuses themselves were given up by the NUS have been lost. But there could still be other such opportunities.

24. With that and since the new year of 1988 is only a few weeks upon us and if I keep this up for much longer, the new year of the Dragon would be upon us, I will, in contrariness to what I have just been saying, wish you, in the words of Bernard to Sir Humphrey: "a happy, change free New Year".

HERMAN R. HOCHSTADT
Guest-of-Honour

Index